Wounds of Love

Wounds of Love

The Story of Saint Padre Pio

Phillip Campbell

TAN Books
Gastonia, North Carolina

Cover design by David Ferris—www.davidferrisdesign.com.

Cover image by Jim Starr.

Interior illustrations by Blueberry Illustrations
www.blueberryillustrations.com.

Library of Congress Control Number: 2022937734

ISBN: 978-1-5051-2319-7
Kindle ISBN: 978-1-5051-2320-3
ePUB ISBN: 978-1-5051-2321-0

Published in the United States by
TAN Books
PO Box 269
Gastonia, NC 28053

www.TANBooks.com

To my son Phillip on the occasion of his confirmation

Contents

Preface

You are about to read about one of the most fascinating saints of modern times, the great Saint Padre Pio of Pietrelcina.

Writing a book on the life of a saint like Padre Pio is extremely challenging. When I started the research for this book, I was overwhelmed by all the information I found. Saint Pio was involved in so many different things: his vocation as a priest, confessor, and spiritual director that changed the lives of thousands; his work founding the great hospital Casa Sollievo della Sofferenza; the troubles he continually had with Rome; the spiritual struggles and suffering he endured relating to the stigmata; the foundation of international "Padre Pio Prayer Groups"; his miracles, his battles with the devil, his personal life with family and friends, and his monastic observance as a Capuchin friar. There was so much the man accomplished!

It soon became clear that a traditional biography would not be possible—there were just too many things to include in a book this size! I ended up having to pick and choose what aspects of Saint Pio's life to incorporate. I was able to include a little bit of everything, but I also had to leave out a lot. So, please don't be sad if your favorite Padre Pio story didn't make it in!

As you read, remember this book is not a biography of Saint Padre Pio; it is historical fiction based on his life. *Historical fiction* is a funny phrase—"historical" and "fiction" seem to be contradictory words. What does the phrase mean? Well, first you should know that all the stories told in this book truly happened: Pio really took a little girl's ribbon and cut it up when he was a boy; he was truly seen in the sky by US pilots during World War II; he really exorcised a screaming woman in church, using the Blessed Sacrament. Yet to tell these stories, I had to use my imagination to fill in the gaps describing *how* they happened. A lot of names of random friars are made up, and most of the conversations are imagined, though whenever possible, I used Padre Pio's actual words as found in his letters and the stories written about him. The compilation of essays on Pio published by the Franciscan Friars of the Immaculate under the title *Padre Pio: The Wonder Worker* was most helpful.

Also, some of the details about Pio's life have been rearranged. For example, the dream narrated in chapter 2 when Pio was eight years old actually happened when he was fourteen. The exorcism depicted in chapter 13 when Pio was elderly really happened twenty years earlier. I wrote that Padre Pio came up with the idea for his hospital during his first suspension, but he really came up with it much earlier. This rearrangement was necessary to take all the different aspects of Padre Pio's marvelous life and help them flow better as a story told in book form.

So, while this book is faithful to the life of Padre Pio, it is not a "history book"; this should not be used as a source or reference for Pio's life. I do, however, hope it inspires you to greater devotion to this amazing saint. In an age that was increasingly becoming enamored with modern thinking and modern technology, Saint Padre Pio served as a "sign of contradiction" (cf. Lk 2:34) reminding the world that Jesus Christ is the same yesterday, today, and forever.

CHAPTER 1

The House of Forgione

"Che sole!" exclaimed Grazio. "What a fierce sun! Time for a break."

He leaned upon his scythe and stood upright, hand on his waist, arching his sore back. He looked aloft at the endless blue sky and squinted at the sun. The afternoon heat in Campania could be relentless. Sweat drained down the peasant's leathery cheeks.

Grazio produced a dingy handkerchief from his pocket and mopped his brow. He turned and looked at his son. "How are you holding up, Francesco?"

A young boy, no more than eight years of age, came trotting behind Grazio, dragging a jumbled ball of twine. He was panting heavily.

"That good, eh?" said Grazio with a smile. "Bundling grain is not easy, I know!"

"I'm . . . all right, Papa," Francesco sighed, continuing to breathe heavy.

His father smiled. "You can't fool your papa. Tell you what—how about we finish this row and then take a break?"

Francesco nodded dutifully. Grazio took up his scythe again and swung it before him in a broad arc, slicing a bundle of wheat. Francesco followed along behind with the twine, tying the bundle off and leaving it to sit for threshing.

Schlunk! Schlunk! went the sound of Grazio's scythe each time it sliced through a cluster of wheat stalks. No sooner had Francesco knelt and tied off a bundle than his father had chopped two more. His bony fingers were aching and didn't seem to work right, causing him to fall even further behind. Francesco grunted as he tied off yet another bundle, and a sweat droplet fell from the end of his nose.

Schlunk! Schlunk! Schlunk!

In a few minutes, Grazio had finished the row and flopped down in the tall grass beneath the shade of a venerable old ficus tree. He took a hunk of bread from his side pouch and gnawed on it, grinning at his son. Francesco continued to toil on the bundles his father left, hunched over, tying each one off as quickly as he could. Finally, he finished the row and hurled his aching body into the grass.

"Papa, we've been out here for seven hours already. Can we go back to Pietrelcina now?"

Grazio looked askance at his son. "I'm afraid not. We've got three hours of good daylight left. We've still got to finish a few more rows before we call it a day. You know better than to ask that."

The boy's countenance sank. "Yes, Papa. I'm sorry, Papa." He rolled over in the grass.

"Francesco, my boy, what is the matter? It's not like you to shirk from chores. You know very well the threshing starts next week."

Francesco sat back up. "I know, Papa. I'm not shirking. It's just that, well, since today is the eve of Pentecost, I was wondering if maybe we could go home early?"

Grazio wiped his brow again, pulled an apple from his pouch, and shined it on his pants. "Go home early, eh?" He produced a small knife and sliced the apple, tossing half to his son. "What's on your mind, boy?"

"Well," said Francesco, explaining as he crunched into the apple, "I know the feast day isn't until tomorrow, but I thought we might use some extra time to prepare?"

"Prepare what? Your mother can handle the cooking well enough, and she has Felicita, and Michele is nearby if she needs help. I'm sure the Pentecost dinner will be fine without you."

"No, I mean prepare my soul," Francesco said quietly as he swallowed a big bite of apple.

Grazio stared at his son thoughtfully while chewing the apple. He blinked, swallowed his snack, and with a twinkle in his eyes, said, "Well, Pentecost is certainly an important feast. And one can never be too prepared for Holy Mass. That's what Padre Vincenzo always says, yes?"

"Yes, Father, that's what Padre always says."

Juice dribbled down Grazio's stubbly chin as he took another bite of the apple. "I suppose it's all right," he said, wiping his mouth on his sleeve.

"Oh, really, Papa? We can go early?"

"Yes, yes," answered Grazio, pitching the apple core, standing up, and brushing bits of the earth off his pants. "The bundling work will still be here come Monday. Our field isn't going anywhere. But Francesco, listen, if we leave off today, I'm going to need extra help next week, understand?"

"Of course, Papa! I promise!"

Grazio tussled the boy's hair. "You're a fine lad. Let's return home. Your mother and the others will be happy to see us."

The farmer grabbed his scythe and slung it over his shoulder. Francesco took up his twine and followed.

The town of Pietrelcina was a half-hour walk from the little piece of land worked by Grazio and his family. The way home followed an old country road, paved with flagstones and no wider than a horse cart. The road meandered up prominences and down steep ascents, passing through field and forest on its way to Pietrelcina. The air was cool where the trees provided pockets of dappled shade. Grazio whistled while they walked, his scythe slung over his shoulder. The day had been hard, but in moments like this, Francesco felt grateful for his father and their way of life.

"Shall we pray a Rosary, Papa?"

"Ah, want to start preparing right away, do you son?" Grazio quipped.

Francesco's father pulled a rosary from his pants pocket. Francesco nodded and did the same.

"*In nómine Patris, et Fílii, et Spíritus Sancti.* Amen."

Francesco made the sign of the cross. "*Credo in unum Deum,*" he began, leading the Credo. Despite his young age, the Rosary was a daily practice for him. He had been acquainted with these prayers for as long as he could remember.

For the better part of twenty minutes, father and son strolled down the country path together to Pietrelcina, holding no conversation save the exchange of Pater Nosters, Ave Marías, and Gloria Patris that made up the rhythm of the Rosary. When they got to the third Glorious Mystery, the Descent of the Holy Spirit, Francesco prayed with special focus, remembering the feast day that would soon be upon them. As they prayed, a gentle breeze blew down from the slopes in the distance and passed across them on the path. Francesco imagined the Holy Spirit blowing on the disciples in the upper room on the first Pentecost. He enjoyed imagining himself in the stories of Scripture while he prayed.

As Grazio and Francesco were concluding the Rosary, the road emerged from the trees and opened into a broad field overlooking the town of Pietrelcina. A cluster of humble houses were gathered around a crumbling medieval castle situated on a gentle hillside. Its streets were narrow, winding, and lined in cobblestone. The houses were low and squat; most homes in Campania were, as it made them less susceptible to earthquakes. It was a rustic, shabby little town that many would consider little more than a hovel. But Francesco had never known any other home, and to him the sight of Pietrelcina's tiny houses and familiar red-tile roofs was as beautiful as Eden.

The pair finished the Rosary as they entered town along the main lane.

"Francesco, since we have some extra time, let's pay a visit to the Brambillas. Mr. Brambilla broke his hand, and he's been out of work for a bit. We should see if they need anything. I promise we will only stay a moment."

"Yes, Papa. I hope Andrianella will be about."

Though it was still only mid-afternoon, other day laborers from the surrounding fields were starting to trickle into town. Grazio and Francesco were not the only two workers the stifling sun had convinced to come in early.

"Hey, Grazio Forgione! How is this fine day treating you, my friend?" one man called out.

"Another day with breath in my lungs is a good day!" Grazio responded cheerfully. Francesco smiled. Everyone seemed to love his father.

Grazio stopped at a market stall to buy a wheel of cheese before heading to the east side of town where the Brambillas lived in a sturdy brick house near the Chiesa Sant'Anna, the parish where Francesco and his family attended Mass. Mr. Brambilla was a shoemaker and an old friend of Grazio's from their youth. Francesco, too, was a friend to Andrianella, the only child of Mr. and Mrs. Brambilla. As they approached the house, Francesco was pleased to see his friend sitting on the porch, sewing a dress.

"*Buon pomeriggio*, good afternoon, Andrianella," said Grazio. "I'm here to call on your mother and father. Are they home?"

"Yes, Mr. Forgione, but Papa is still hurt," answered Andrianella, never looking up from her needlework.

"Ah, I thought so, but that's why I have come—and I've brought your mother some cheese!" Grazio held up the wheel and smiled.

Andrianella finally looked up. She offered a smile in return. "She'll like that. Go on in."

Grazio nodded. "Francesco, stay out here and play with Andrianella. I'll only be a moment."

He leaned his scythe against the wall of the house and went in, cheese in hand, leaving the two children outside, an awkward silence hanging over them like a cloud. Andrianella and Francesco had always played together, but she was two years his senior and had begun to act aloof. She continued to focus on her needlework, ignoring Francesco.

"What are you working on?" the boy finally asked.

"What does it look like, Francesco? A dress. My Nonna gave me this pretty red satin band for Pentecost, and I am going to sew it onto my dress."

"It is very pretty."

Andrianella snorted. "What do you know about dresses?"

Francesco shrugged and did not work up the courage to speak again as several minutes passed in silence. He was grateful when his father emerged from the home a few moments later. "Ready to go, Son?"

"Yes, Father," the boy said eagerly. "*Ciao*, Andrianella."

The girl did not respond, continuing her project as if Francesco did not exist.

After they had put some distance between them and the Brambillas' house, Francesco said, "Father, why has Andrianella been so cross these last few times I have seen her?"

"She's ten going on eleven, no? That can be a tricky time for girls. I think maybe you will understand when you get a bit older."

Francesco considered this. He admitted that could be true.

"And perhaps she is anxious about her father. For a shoemaker to break his hand is a big deal. No hand, no work. No work, no money. No money, no food. Let us remember to pray for them this day."

A few minutes later, father and son reached the small stone house on the edge of town that the Forgione family called home. It was built into the side of a hill with one side facing the town and the other open to the fields outside Pietrelcina.

"Mamma Peppa, we are home!" called Grazio as they walked in.

A thin woman with dark hair and piercing brown eyes emerged from the kitchen. She held a wooden cooking ladle in one hand, while her other supported a chubby baby girl.

"You're early," she said, her tone one of disapproval.

"What did I say? I told you she'd be happy to see us!" Grazio whispered, nudging Francesco with his elbow. Then turning to his wife, "Aye. The sun was fierce today, and Francesco wanted to come home." Grazio kissed his wife and took the little child in his arms, tickling her affectionately. "He wanted to spend some time preparing for tomorrow's Mass."

A smile curled across Mamma Peppa's wiry lips. "Is that so? Well, Francesco, please go feed the donkey, and then you may have all the time you need. Supper won't be ready for some time yet."

"Thank you, Mama," Francesco said, kissing his mother on the cheek before walking toward the creaking trap door in the floor of the main room. This revealed a ladder that provided access to the storeroom on the ground floor where the Forgiones' donkey was stabled. The dirt-floored storeroom opened out into the backyard and the fields beyond that spread out below Pietrelcina. The shabby animal blinked at Francesco from behind his pen as the boy scuttled down the ladder.

"Hello, Zio, my friend."

He scooped up an armful of alfalfa grass with a pitchfork and stuffed it into the donkey's feeding trough. Zio stuck his snout into the trough and began to munch as Francesco sat down in the pile of alfalfa and against the stone wall of the storeroom. The stones were cool on his sweaty back.

Francesco sighed and looked out toward the sun-tinted clouds grazing atop the verdant fields that stretched beyond Pietrelcina. He closed his eyes and breathed deeply, finally feeling a sense of peace.

"Come, Holy Spirit, fill the hearts of your faithful and kindle in me the fire of your love," he prayed. "Prepare me, O Lord, for thy feast tomorrow. Prepare me to receive you."

As he prayed, Francesco imagined his heart being lit on fire and God blowing on it, the way he and his brother sometimes blew on the kindling to get a fire started in the oven.

He imagined the breath of God to be the Holy Spirit. The thought made him feel warm and happy.

Gradually, Francesco's words fell silent as the images, prayers, and feelings all merged into one. In his reverie, he lost track of time. It felt like things were happening, but he did not understand what. Peace filled him like water filling a bucket.

"Francesco," a thin voice called to him.

Francesco opened his eyes. In the storehouse doorway stood another boy, curly-haired with dark, vacant eyes. He blocked out the sun and cast a cold shadow over the room.

"Francesco, aren't you upset the way Andrianella treated you?"

Francesco hesitated, caught off guard by the boy's sudden presence, but answered, "She has good reason to be cross. Her father is hurt. Her family is having a hard time."

"No, no, no, that's not it at all," replied the dark-eyed boy. "The real reason is she thinks you're dumb. Doesn't that make you angry?"

"Go away," said Francesco stiffly. "I'm trying to pray."

The boy moved closer, casting his shadow over Francesco and sending a shiver through his body. "Didn't you hear me? Andrianella thinks you're dumb. She thinks you're a *stupido*. Everybody thinks you're a *stupido*."

"They can think what they want, but I know you are lying."

"Nobody really likes you. They only pretend to like you. Nobody likes a *stupido* like you."

"In the name of Jesus Christ, get away from me!" Francesco yelled, making the sign of the cross. "Virgin Mother, hide me under your mantle," he added, clasping his rosary.

The dark-eyed boy scowled and stepped back as if intimidated but trying not to show it. "We'll talk again some other time, Francesco." He slowly backed out of the storeroom, keeping his gaze on him.

"Come again, and I'll tell you the same thing again," Francesco said defiantly. He was no longer afraid but felt empowered by the names of Jesus and the Blessed Mother. "But before you go, I have one question for you."

"Oh? Please . . . go right ahead."

"Do you know who the real *stupido* is? *You*!" Francesco held his rosary aloft and pointed the crucifix at the dark-haired boy. The fiendish boy let out a foul, gurgling noise. His body began to dissipate into the air like smoke rising from a fire.

"I am so sick of that boy," Francesco muttered as he closed his eyes and continued his prayers. Slowly, the peace of the moment returned.

Sometime later, Francesco was roused by the sound of sheep and footsteps approaching the storeroom. It was his elder brother, Michele. Francesco made the sign of the cross and leapt up from the alfalfa pile.

"Aye, *pécore*, *pécore*! C'mon, *pécore*!" Michele called, corralling the family's sheep into an enclosure behind the Forgione's house with his walking stick. Five years his elder, Michele was a full head taller than Francesco. At thirteen, he seemed powerful and confident. Behind him was their little sister, Felicita, two years younger than Francesco.

"C'mon, *pécore*!" she called, mimicking her elder brother. The Forgione flock was not large, only a dozen, but it was enough. At age eight, Francesco was only now beginning to have a vague idea of the social divisions of the world. He knew his family was not poor, but he also realized that poverty was not too many steps below them.

"Francesco! I am surprised you are home already," said Michele, closing the gate to the enclosure.

"Papa said we could come home early to prepare for Pentecost!"

Mamma Peppa's shrill voice came ringing from the kitchen. "Francesco, is that your brother and sister? Tell them dinner is ready! *Mangia*!"

The three children entered the storeroom and scrambled up the ladder into the house. Mamma and Papa were already seated at the creaky old table, along with three-year-old Pellegrina, Francesco's other sister. The baby, Grazia, was slumbering peacefully on a sack of flour in the corner.

Though the Forgione's did not have a lot, Mamma Peppa knew how to stretch what they had. The food was often simple but was always enough. Tonight, it was *acquacotta*—a brothy soup made with onion, tomato, and chunks of breadcrusts left over from the week. Dinner began, as always, with Grazio leading the family in prayer. When he was finished, Mamma Peppa exclaimed, "*Mangia*! *Pensa di niente*! Don't think, just eat!!"

As they ate, Papa Grazio discussed the harvest, the Brambillas, and the weather, while Mamma Peppa talked about her day, the health of her parents, and her plans for the Pentecost feast tomorrow. The younger children listened while they ate, while Michele and Francesco sometimes joined the conversation. As was the case in many Italian households, dinner at the Forgiones' was always loud and boisterous.

After dinner, the family gathered around the hearth, their dispositions turning more solemn. Grazio, seated in a chair, puffed on a pipe while holding little Pellegrina on his lap. Francesco, Michele, and Felicita sat cross-legged on the floor, while Mamma Peppa nursed baby Grazia.

As darkness fell outside, Mamma Peppa said, "Fetch your rosaries, children." Francesco and his siblings obeyed and returned, beads in hand, to kneel before an image of Our Lady of Perpetual Help. Grazio knelt, too, beside Francesco, smiling at the boy with a twinkle in his eye. Francesco smiled back. Nobody knew they had already prayed the Rosary that day, but it was no matter. Francesco loved the Rosary and was happy to pray it again.

"*In nómine Patris, et Fílii, et Spíritus Sancti,*" began Grazio.

"Amen," the family intoned.

Thus went things in the house of Forgione.

CHAPTER 2

The True Battle

FRANCESCO'S HEART WAS lifted as he listened to the singing of the beautiful Pentecost sequence. "*Veni, Sancte Spíritus, et emítte caelítus Lucis tuæ rádium*—come, Holy Spirit, send forth the heavenly ray of your light."

He loved the Pentecost liturgy at Chiesa Sant'Anna: the "*Veni Sancte Spíritus,*" Padre Vincenzo's red vestments, the dramatic retelling of the coming of the Holy Ghost. But Francesco's favorite part of the Pentecost Mass was when a pair of boys scrambled up into the balcony overlooking the nave and showered rose petals upon the congregation, symbolizing the tongues of fire which descended upon the Apostles that day in the upper room.

The Forgione family took an entire pew to themselves, and not comfortably—Pellegrina and baby Grazia had to be held for everyone else to squeeze in. Kneeling was a challenge, and Francesco could barely fold his hands to pray without his elbows jostling those of Michele or Felicita. Still, these minor discomforts were nothing compared to the graces available through the Sacrifice of the Mass. From his earliest years, Francesco's mother had taught him to respect the Mass with reverent awe.

"In the Holy Mass, the sacrifice of the Lord Jesus is presented to God for our salvation," she had told him. "It is through Mass that all the graces of Our Lord's suffering are given to us."

When Padre Vincenzo held the host aloft during the consecration, Francesco liked to imagine rays of light beaming forth from it—from the host, out into the church, and then extending to the entire world, flooding everything in grace.

When the moment came to receive the Lord, Francesco knelt devoutly at the altar rail. "*Corpus Dómini nostri Jesu Christi custódiat ánimam tuam in vitam ætérnam. Amen,*" Padre Vincenzo said, placing Jesus on the boy's tongue. Francesco imagined himself receiving fire into his mouth—the very fire of God's life. Sometimes, he even thought he truly saw the host glowing with otherworldly radiance. In Francesco's day, it was not common for a boy so young to receive Holy Communion, but Padre Vincenzo had admitted Francesco at an earlier age because of the extraordinary devotion he held for the Blessed Sacrament.

When Mass was over, the family spent a few moments lingering in the church to pray before filing out into the cobblestone streets of Pietrelcina. Francesco blinked in the afternoon sun, which was often so bright when leaving the church. The sky was deep blue, not a cloud in sight. All around, families were laughing and talking about their plans for the day. Michele had already sauntered off to find some of his friends. Francesco felt happy and at peace.

"Papa," he said, tugging his father's trousers, "can I go play with some of the boys?"

"Of course, lad. But don't be out for too long. Today, we are feasting!"

"Yes, Papa!"

Francesco ran down the lane toward a group of boys playing ball.

"Eh! Francesco is here to play!" one of the boys called, waving.

Unconcerned that he was still in his church clothes, Francesco joined the game, kicking an old worn football up and down the lane. The boys dashed to and fro, shouting and kicking the leather-wrapped pig bladder that served as the ball. Francesco laughed as he played. His life seldom allowed for carefree times like this.

One of the boys kicked the ball toward Francesco.

"Francesco, it's coming your way!" called Georgio. Francesco lunged, but it passed between his thin little legs and went rolling down the street out into the square. An older boy began cursing at Francesco for missing the kick.

"I'm sorry!" said Francesco sheepishly. "I'll fetch it."

"Leave him alone," said Giorgio to the older boy. "He's only eight."

The older boy smacked Giorgio upside the head and unleashed a torrent of abuse and blasphemies upon him for talking back. Giorgio grew angry and shouted at the older boy, blaspheming and cursing as well. Francesco stood still as if paralyzed, watching the boys cuss and blaspheme—and still in their church clothes! He began to shake. His lip quivered. His stomach sank. He turned and ran from the street, out into the square, passing the ball and continuing onward.

"Hey, *stupido*! Aren't you even going to get the ball?" the older boy called after him.

Francesco did not hear. He was already a block away, panting hard with tears welling in his eyes. He found a wooden gate that led into an alley and quickly ducked in behind it. He crunched himself up into a ball, knees pulled up to his chin, and wept. Big tears stung his eyes and rolled down his cheeks as his little body convulsed.

He must have sat there for a half hour at least. His crying eventually subsided into sniffling. Now calmer, he made the sign of the cross and clasped his hands in prayer.

"Dear Jesus," he said tearfully, "forgive their blasphemy."

Suddenly, he heard footsteps approaching. "Francesco, are you back there?"

It was Mamma Peppa.

Francesco came out from behind the gate and flung himself into his mother's arms, soaking her dress in more tears.

"*Amore mio*! My sweet boy, what is the matter?" Mamma Peppa held him and patted his hair, saying his name sweetly.

"Why do they take God's name in vain, Mama?" he finally said, his face still buried in her dress. "The boys were taking God's name in vain."

"Ah, I see," said Mamma Peppa gently, rubbing his back. "The world is a cold, unloving place sometimes, is it not? People forget God and His honor."

"Mama," he said sniffling, looking up at her with bleary eyes. "Not a half hour before I saw that older boy receive Jesus on his tongue in Holy Mass. He used that same tongue to blaspheme. I just couldn't bear the thought of that. It was so sad, Mama."

She looked at him sadly but with a mother's pride. "Ah, my little saint, come, let's go home and celebrate Pentecost. I am making some dove bread and a leg of lamb. Does that sound good?"

"Yes, Mama, but may I have a little while longer?"

"Of course, *amore*. You sit behind this gate for as long as you need to. Just be home before it gets too late."

Francesco nodded dutifully. Mamma Peppa kissed his forehead and left the boy alone with his thoughts.

Francesco sat behind the wooden gate for some time, pondering what had happened.

If they dishonor God's name, I will make it up by praising God even more.

He began repeating little prayers to himself that he had known since he was very young.

"*Sit nomen Dómini benedíctum*—may the name of the Lord be blessed!" he said as he pulled himself to his feet and walked out into the lanes of Pietrelcina again. "May the Most Blessed Sacrament be praised and adored forever," he repeated, crossing himself as he passed by Chiesa Sant'Anna. "May the Holy Trinity be blessed now and forever!" he said as he turned down the narrow lane that led toward his home.

He went on in this way, with little prayers that he hurled up to heaven accompanying his trip home, until he passed by the Brambilla house. Andrianella was again seated on the front porch, still working on the red satin band. Her mind was deeply engrossed in her work; so much so that she took no notice of Francesco. He paused and furrowed his brow.

"What are you doing?" he said curtly.

She girl looked up, irritated. "Boy, are you daft! I told you yesterday, I'm attaching this red band to my dress."

"But it's Sunday! *Pentecost* Sunday!"

"Of course it is! My Nonno and Nonna are coming over tonight for the feast! They will be staying for a few days to help with Papa. I need to finish working on this so I can wear the dress for dinner, so I don't have time to talk to *you*."

Francesco's lip began to quiver again. The sadness he had felt earlier came flooding back.

"But Andrianella Brambilla, you know better than to work on Sunday! Stop immediately! You are offending God!"

The girl stared at him with icy eyes. Francesco stared back, full of indignation, his little body shaking. Andrienella broke the silence with a scornful snort.

"You are slow in the brain, Francesco."

She went back to sewing.

Something inside Francesco snapped. He pounced forward and snatched the dress from the girl's lap. He tore the red satin band off, undoing her entire day's work.

"Francesco! You buffoon!"

She lunged at him, but the boy dodged swiftly. Throwing the dress on the ground, he snatched a pair of scissors out of Andrianella's sewing box and sliced the satin band into pieces. Andrianella shrieked, clutched her hair, and stomped in fury.

Francesco flung the pieces at her. "Keep holy the Lord's day!" he said coldly, hurling the scissors to the ground. Francesco fully expected a slap across the face, but instead Andrianella burst into tears and ran into her house. Francesco was left alone in the street, the Pentecost dress and fragments of red satin laying on the ground before him.

What have I done?

He did not have time to reflect, for not a minute later there came a commotion from inside the Brambillas' house. The noise shook him out of his trance. He bolted home, running faster than he'd ever run before. It seemed as though he was flying, running through a dream, the cobblestone street nothing but a blur beneath his feet. His heart pounded so hard he felt like it would burst out of his chest.

When he got home, he did not come in the front door. Rather, he scrambled down the slope to the back of the house, leapt over the sheep enclosure, ran into the storeroom, and threw himself face first into the alfalfa pile. Then he sobbed, now for the second time today, but more violently than before. He thought about his pious resolutions earlier and how proud he was of himself. Now, he felt dumb for thinking it would be so easy. Zio the donkey stared at Francesco blankly, understanding nothing but hoping he might get fed.

It was not long before Mrs. Brambilla called upon Mamma Peppa. Francesco could not hear what they were saying from the storeroom, but he knew the substance of the conversation. He could hear how agitated Mrs. Brambilla was and could sense the disappointment in his mother's tone. But the worst was not what he heard but what he did not hear—nothing from his father. He wondered what his father must think about all this.

He heard the door close upstairs and the voices subside. A moment later, the trapdoor to the upstairs creaked open. He expected his father to come down the ladder with a switch to whip him with, but it was Mamma Peppa. Francesco sat upright, sniffling.

"Mama, I . . ."

THWACK! Mamma Peppa's wooden spoon smacked the side of his head.

"Arghh!" Francesco grimaced.

"Whatsa'matter with you, eh? Who do you think you are? Do you have any idea how upset Andrianella and Mrs. Brambilla are? You have dishonored old friends of our family, and you've made your father and I look like bad parents!"

"You're not bad parents, Mama!"

"Who made you lord and master over that girl's conduct?" Mamma Peppa continued, waving her arms. "Are you her older brother? Are you her father? No! You're just a neighborhood boy who had no business touching that girl's dress."

"But Mama—"

"But *nothing*, Francesco. You can't just lose your composure every time you see something you disapprove of. If you do, you'll never be happy! What kind of life would that be?"

"But Mama," he protested, "she was working on the Lord's Day!"

"Oh, and because you cut up a little girl's satin ribbon, that makes you holy?"

"Well . . . no, Mama, but she was offending God by working on Sunday."

"And by ruining the band her grandmother gave her and throwing her dress on the ground, you are pleasing God? How does this show the love of God?"

Francesco considered that for a moment. "God is love, but he is also justice, no?"

Mamma Peppa's countenance softened. "You are right, Francesco, of course. God is loving but also just."

Francesco buried his head in his hands. "I'm sorry I disappointed you, Mama."

Mamma Peppa knelt beside her son and grabbed his shoulders. "Francesco, remember the Gospel? 'How can you say to your brother, "Let me take the speck out of your eye," when there is a beam in your own eye? First remove the beam from your own eye, only then can you remove the speck from your brother's eye.'"

"My own eye?"

"You cannot control what other people do. You cannot stop those boys from blaspheming. You cannot stop Andrianella from sewing on Sunday. You cannot stop the sins of the world. There's only one thing you can control." She pressed her bony finger into the boy's chest. "*Yourself.* You only have control over yourself, Francesco. You are the only one you need to control. Pray, speak the truth in love, then leave the rest to God."

With that, she turned and ascended the ladder back into the house. "Oh, you're also working every afternoon this week at the Brambillas' in reparation for the satin. Mr. Brambilla could really use the help while he rccovers."

"Yes, Mama," Francesco groaned. He would have rather been whipped a hundred times than have to see Andrianella again.

The Forgione's Pentecost dinner was somber that night. Papa was quiet. *Too* quiet. It was not until after the family was finishing up the meal that Grazio said, "I think it's time Francesco started working with the flock in the fields. Michele is old enough to hire himself out as a laborer in town, and I can manage the field alone until Felicita gets a little older. Learning to pasture the sheep will be good for you, Francesco."

"Shall I take him out in the morning to show him how it's done, Father?" asked Michele.

"I think Francesco knows his way around the sheep," Grazio answered. "I will take him out in the morning myself."

A few hours later, Francesco lay awake in the dark, listening to his brother snore and thinking about the day. He and Michele slept in a small room off the side of the kitchen, sharing a straw mattress on a rugged wooden frame. All Francesco could see in his mind's eye were the angry faces of Andrianella and his mother.

He sat up in bed and looked out the window. The sky was clear and starry with a crescent moon. He could see the broad pastureland sweeping out below the hills of Pietrelcina. The fields were quiet under the watchful stars. Winding along the side of the field, he could see the little stone road that led to the Piana Romana, the name of the field worked by his father. In the dim moonlight, the road gleamed like a white ribbon across the countryside.

A ribbon, Francesco thought. It reminded him of Andrianella.

He got up from his bed and lay down on the floor, his head resting on nothing but the clammy stone in an act of penance. He huddled up and began repeating, "Lord Jesus Christ, Son of God, have mercy on me, a sinner." After some time, he drifted off into a fitful sleep plagued by a vivid dream. A man stood over him, luminous and majestic, glowing like the moon, full of power and radiance. He took Francesco's hand, saying, "Come with me, for you must fight a tough and aggressive warrior."

The man whisked Francesco away, and suddenly they seemed to be standing on the plains below Pietrelcina. Francesco became aware of the presence of many others standing around him, all equally radiant, clothed in white, and exceedingly beautiful, both men and women. But across the plain loomed another figure, tall and imposing with dark eyes. Behind him was arrayed a horde of repulsive characters—Francesco was unsure if they were monsters or merely deformed people.

Francesco's guide pointed at the dark figure and said, "You will have to do battle with him."

Francesco shrunk back. "I cannot possibly defeat an enemy that big!"

"You must fight with him," his guide said reassuringly. "You will fight, and you will win. Take heart. Enter the combat with confidence. Go forth courageously. I shall be with you. In reward for your victory over him, I will give you a shining crown to adorn your brow."

The man's words seemed to seep into Francesco, flowing through his veins and giving him confidence. Francesco shouted and charged the enemy. The dark-eyed character roared and lunged for Francesco, fuming smoke from his fearsome jaws. But Francesco was not daunted; he made a fist and struck the dark figure. The enemy immediately came unraveled as if the entirety of his dark, hulking form were nothing but a pile of blankets. The blankets fell to the earth, revealing a scrawny, pathetic creature hiding within. It shrieked and ran, scampering away, lizard-like, across the plains. The hideous army that had been flanking the man evaporated as a shout of triumph went up from the luminous white-clad host on the plain.

Francesco's father woke him before sunrise. The two ate a silent breakfast of crusty bread and cheese before climbing down the ladder to the storeroom and walking out into the sheep pen.

"Aye, *pécore*, *pécore*! C'mon, *pécore*!" Grazio called to the sheep. The flock perked their heads and crowded around Grazio, eager to be led out.

Francesco really did not need much guidance on how to shepherd the flock; he had been out with Michele and his father many times. He assumed the real reason his father wanted to come was to speak with him privately. But Grazio said nothing as the two led the flock out of the enclosure and down the sloping hillside onto the plains.

The fields around Pietrelcina were common grazing land used by many of the locals. Across the hillsides everywhere, he could see shepherds leading lines of sheep out for grazing. Many of them were acquaintances of the Forgiones.

"Hey, Grazio!" one called. "How's life for the Forgiones?"

"Very well, my brother!" Grazio replied. Francesco smiled at seeing his father be so friendly. Maybe he was not as angry as he thought.

Grazio and Francesco walked as the sun rose higher, turning the sky from pinkish orange to yellow, its rays sweeping over the plains. They arrived at a grassy knoll, a spot where the Forgiones were accustomed to grazing their little flock. Grazio handed Francesco the shepherd's staff he used to guide the sheep.

"Good luck, my boy. Stay here till late afternoon, bring the flock home, then go see Mrs. Brambilla for work."

"Yes, Papa."

His father smiled. "You know Francesco, the true battle is against yourself."

Grazio walked off, whistling into the morning air.

CHAPTER 3

Too Much to Leave You that Way

In the passing years, the fields around Pietrelcina became Francesco's second home, the Forgione flock his constant companions. The sunny blue vault of heaven became the roof over his head, the breezy field grass, a verdant carpet beneath his feet. In the summer, his skin was tanned by the sun as he meandered over the meadows. Campanian winters were mild, snowing only occasionally and seldom more than a dusting on the pastures. On such days, Francesco and the flock huddled beneath the boughs of a venerable old elm tree that stood solitary like a sentinel watching over Pietrelcina's fields.

When Francesco's parents sent him into these fields, Mamma Peppa told him he was to spend his alone time profitably.

"Many people get restless when they are on their own," she had said. "They can't bear to be alone with their thoughts—and with God. But not so with you!"

She had given him a little stack of books to practice his reading while in the fields.

"Strengthen your mind and spirit."

Francesco always brought his books with him, studying with his back to the old elm tree. When he could find time, he attended classes in a little stone schoolhouse in Pietrelcina with other young people. He was one of the most attentive and diligent students.

Over the years, Francesco never forgot what his father had told him after he had ruined Andrianella's ribbon and dress.

"The true battle is against yourself."

The hours alone gave Francesco endless opportunities to reflect on his father's words. How easy it was to make a good resolution but how difficult to carry it out! Francesco was slowly learning that mastering one's own selfish impulses was the greatest struggle any person must face. He tried to use his time in the fields to better himself with prayer and reflection. Padre Vincenzo had told Francesco the story of Saint Patrick of Ireland—how Patrick had also been a shepherd as a boy and spent his time in prayer, sometimes praying a hundred times per day and a hundred times per night! Inspired by this, Francesco would fashion little crosses of wood, plant them in the earth, and kneel in prayer before them.

One blustery spring day, Francesco was kneeling before one of his wooden crosses while the flock grazed nearby. He had been working hard to memorize some of the psalms of David.

"The Lord is my shepherd, I shall want for nothing . . ."

As he was praying, two older boys, cigarettes in hand, approached, their flocks following obediently behind. Francesco paused momentarily, a little self-conscious of what they would think of him. He shook it off, however, closed his eyes, and continued his prayer.

"He hath set me in a place of pasture. He hath brought me up, on the water of refreshment . . ."

As their footsteps grew nearer, Francesco waited for their mockery. But instead, the boys threw down their cigarettes and knelt behind Francesco, praying silently with him until he had finished the psalm. Francesco learned two things that day: one, to never judge someone based on how they look, and two, that he could have an influence on others and draw them closer to God.

Several months after that morning, in the peak of the summer heat, Francesco's father stirred him awake.

"Get up boy, you will not be working in the fields today."

"Why not, Papa?" Francesco asked, wiping the sleep from his eyes.

"Because today, we are going to Saint Pellegrino. Hurry and get ready, it is a long journey."

"Yes, Papa!"

The Shrine of Saint Pellegrino in Avellino was a three-hour journey south. After a quick breakfast, they harnessed

Zio to the old farm wagon and began the bumpy ride along the stony road.

"Papa, who was Saint Pellegrino?"

"Saint Pellegrino was a martyr from Roman times. He refused to worship the Roman emperor on his birthday. He and some companions were tortured and put to death."

"Why are we going to his shrine?"

"Well, my boy, today is his feast day, and he is very beloved by the people of Pietrelcina. I want to ask his prayers for the harvest this fall."

Francesco sensed that his father wanted to say more but had stopped himself short.

"And?" the boy said.

"Can you guess how old Pellegrino was when he was put to death?"

"I don't know. Was he a nobleman? Or a cleric?"

"He was just a common boy. Probably about your age."

"What did they do to him?" Francesco asked.

"Many horrible things. They beat him. Flogged him. Burned him. Beheaded him."

Francesco looked off, gazing blankly at the patchwork of green fields passing by the wagon. He tried to picture the spectacle—a boy his own age, enduring all the torments of Roman cruelty.

"How could he handle all that?" Francesco asked, turning back to his father.

"They say that those who suffer for Christ receive special graces to endure their trial. Christ suffered the cross. Everyone who wants to follow Christ will have his own cross too. It might not be like the torment of Saint Pellegrino, but it will be a cross, nonetheless."

Francesco thought long and hard about this. Over the past few years, he had made it a practice to offer his own little sufferings to God for the salvation of sinners—the aching in his stomach when he felt the pangs of hunger, the sting of the summer sunburn on his neck, his stiff cold fingers in the winter, the little irritations and misunderstandings that often arose in large families. But compared to the story of Saint Pellegrino, these seemed like nothing. What if he was ever called to suffer like Saint Pellegrino? Would he have it in him? What was it like to truly suffer for Christ?

"Truth be told," Grazio continued, "your mother and I have been impressed with your growth these past few years. You're an honest, hard-working, and intelligent boy. Your piety is very . . ." his father seemed to be searching for the right word, "shall we say, very *unique*. And mature for a boy of your age. Saint Pellegrino was probably a lot like you. His prayers will help you find your place in life."

The sanctuary of Saint Pellegrino was in Altavilla Irpina, a sleepy hillside town like Pietrelcina. As Grazio and Francesco arrived around noon, they could see many other travelers making their way toward the village.

"Saint Pellegrino is popular!" exclaimed Francesco.

"He is indeed. August 25 is always a major pilgrimage day for the town. There will probably be a few thousand pilgrims here today."

"A few thousand!" Francesco was impressed. Being from little Pietrelcina, he had never seen even one thousand people together at once. He wondered how big of a crowd that must be.

He would soon find out. The Baroque-era shrine in the center of town was teaming with pilgrims. Francesco and his father found it a challenge to simply get into the narthex. Besides the pilgrims, the lane beside the church was crowded with beggars seeking alms. A few town constables attempted to keep the order as the unending flow of people pressed to get into the shrine.

Unfortunately, inside was no better. Francesco and Grazio were packed shoulder to shoulder, not so much walking as being pushed with the ebb and flow of the crowd. The pilgrims came from many different places and states in life: from towns all over came men, women, children, poor people, and well-to-do people. They all milled around, trying to get to the front of the church to pay their respects to the saint's altar—a surging, sweaty mass of humanity eager to lay some of life's burdens before the image of Saint Pellegrino.

Francesco and Grazio eventually had their turn before the altar. They knelt and prayed briefly before being shuffled off to the side. But thankfully, Grazio found an empty pew where father and son were able to spend more time in quiet prayer.

All around their bowed heads, the flow of pilgrims continued unceasingly. Francesco peeked up at one point and saw a woman carrying a toddler with a severe physical handicap, his legs below the knee twisted unnaturally, his feet curled up like claws. As she made her way to the front of the shrine, she began to wail.

"Santo Pellegrino! Heal my son! Heal my son! Help my son walk!"

She held the baby aloft before the image of the saint as if presenting him as an offering. Francesco was deeply moved with pity.

"Let us pray for her," said Grazio quietly.

Francesco nodded.

The woman lingered at the altar, weeping and holding her child in the air. Pilgrims behind her were getting impatient, forcing ushers to come move her along. But the woman refused, continuing to cry and howl.

Francesco's father tugged at his sleeve. "Let's get out of here. We don't need to stay for this."

"Let's pray a little longer for her, Papa," Francesco said. His father looked at the woman, then back to him. He nodded.

The ushers laid hands on the mother, ready to forcibly escort her from the church. In an act of furious desperation, she tore free from their clutches, lunged forward, and placed the deformed child directly on top of the saint's altar.

"If you don't want to cure him, take him yourself! I don't want him!"

A murmur of shock and disapproval spread throughout the crowds.

"Throw her out!" a man jeered.

But suddenly, the crowd fell silent and gasped, for to the astonishment of all, the child stood upright on his own two legs, no longer warped with deformity but straight and whole.

"Mama!" the boy cried. "I can stand. I can . . . I can walk."

The woman took the child back into her arms, drenching him in tears of joy.

"A miracle!" people began to shout. Crowds from outside grew curious and began to press forward. Grazio grabbed Francesco to leave as clergy, police, and every other passerby piled into the shrine to discover the source of the excitement. It took twenty minutes to sift through the dense crowd and escape to the freedom of the open air.

Grazio pulled his son before his wagging finger. "Francesco, when I say it is time to go, *then it is time to go!* Do you understand me? We could have been crushed to death in there." Francesco was gazing back at the shrine. "Are you listening to me, Francesco?"

The boy finally faced his father. "It was a miracle, Papa! Did you see that? We saw a crippled boy be healed!"

Grazio calmed himself and smiled. "That we did, my boy. We are lucky."

"No, not 'lucky.' We prayed for this. The woman prayed, you and I prayed. Saint Pellegrino prayed, and God heard our prayers."

On the journey home, Francesco considered the power of prayer and the intercession of the saints. It would be a lesson that stayed with him for many, many years.

In autumn of that year, Grazio and Mamma Peppa allowed Francesco's sisters to take over some of the shepherding so he could spend more time in school. He divided his time between the fields and the schoolhouse. He would bring his schoolwork with him to the fields, practicing writing or working out his arithmetic with his back to the old elm he was so fond of. And whenever he could spare a moment, he prayed before one of the many wooden crosses he had set up around the fields. He grew a little taller, his mind a little sharper, his bearing a little more confident.

One warm September day while Francesco was reclining against the elm, practicing his writing, he caught sight of a dark figure meandering up the road toward Pietrelcina. As the figure drew closer, Francesco could see that he was wearing a religious habit of some sort.

"A brother!" he said excitedly.

Tossing his writing book aside into the grass, the boy leapt to his feet and dashed across the sloping meadow, down toward the lane. His sheep saw the boy's movement and instinctively followed him.

"Hello, Brother!" Francesco called out, panting as he approached.

"Peace be with you, lad," greeted the man, tipping a wide-brimmed hat with his free hand, the other grasping a walking stick. He looked to be in his mid-twenties, with a dark complexion and a handsome black beard.

"Are you a Franciscan?" Francesco asked, noting the man's brown habit.

"Yes, in a way," said the man. "I am a Capuchin friar. My name is Brother Camillo. And I can tell what *you* do!"

"Excuse me?" Francesco asked, puzzled.

"You are a shepherd."

"How did you know that?"

"You are surrounded by sheep, boy!" Brother Camillo said with a broad smile. Francesco had not noticed his sheep following him down to the lane, now gathered behind him.

"Oh! Yes, of course! My name is Francesco Forgione. I tend my family's flock when I am not in school."

"Francesco! That's a very good name! A very Franciscan name. Tell me Francesco Forgione, would you accompany me to Pietrelcina?"

"Of course! It would be an honor!"

Francesco walked with Brother Camillo up the lane back toward Pietrelcina, the sheep trailing meekly along. Brother Camillo and Francesco talked along the way. It seemed Brother Camillo had come to Pietrelcina to beg alms for his little monastery. He was a very likable man, simple and humble, with a joyful disposition. Francesco peppered the man with a barrage of questions about the life of a brother: How many times a day did he pray? How long did he have to study to become a Capuchin? How many brothers were at his monastery? Did all Capuchins have beards as nice as his?

"You are a bright, inquisitive boy," said Brother Camillo. "And it's clear you love God very much. Have you ever considered a religious vocation?"

"Me? A vocation? But I'm just a boy."

"You are a bit young, but many of the brothers in our monastery first considered religious life at your age. And remember what God said to Jeremiah the prophet: 'Before I formed you in the womb, I knew you, and before you were born I consecrated you; I appointed you a prophet to the nations.'"

Francesco looked at the ground bashfully. "If I am being honest, I have considered a vocation, but I do not think I am worthy. I am a sinner, and I still struggle with many faults."

"You are a sinner, eh? Well, let me welcome you to the human race! What does our Lord say? 'It is not the healthy who need a doctor, but the sick.'"

Francesco smiled. "I suppose you are right."

Brother Camillo laughed. "Look at me! I have only asked you to walk with me to Pietrelcina, and here I am talking you into religious life. Forgive my forwardness!"

"It's all right, Brother. I like thinking about it."

"Then I will keep you in my prayers as you discern. Remember, Francesco, God loves you just the way you are, but he loves you too much to leave you that way," the friar added with a wink and a smile. "Something tells me he has big plans for you."

As they approached the outskirts of town, Brother Camillo tipped his hat and said, "Good day to you, Francesco Forgione. Thank you for the company. I hope we shall meet again someday. May God reward you."

With that, the friar went into the town, leaving Francesco alone with his sheep. The boy turned and darted back into the meadow, the confused sheep ambling along behind. He felt full of life as he ran and tumbled into the grass, sprawling out on his back and gazing into the azure dome of the heavens. Francesco's heart swelled with happiness; joy was the very breath in his nostrils.

That evening at dinner, Francesco announced, "I want to be a religious brother."

Though he thought it would surprise his family, it appeared they were expecting this announcement.

"That is wonderful, Francesco! Praise God!" said Mamma Peppa.

"Yes indeed!" Grazio said with a grin. "But one question first—your mother tells me you came home today without your writing book. Where is your schoolbook, Francesco?"

"My writing book? Um . . . ah . . ."

He suddenly remembered and hung his head.

"I left it in the field by the elm tree."

His father, wiping his mouth with a handkerchief, said, "After dinner, go get your writing book and bring it back."

"Yes, Papa."

The walk out to the elm tree and back took over an hour. When Francesco returned, night was already falling and the family was settling in for the Rosary. Grazio was sitting in his chair, smoking a pipe.

"Do you have the book?" asked Grazio.

The boy set the book on the kitchen table.

"Good. *Now*, we may talk about you becoming a monk. The first thing a monk needs is attention to detail. No more leaving your schoolbooks out in the fields."

Francesco nodded.

"You will also need to keep up with your schoolwork. I know you are pious, but you need to be educated as well. You may need to devote more time to study, and you must excel at it."

"I know, Papa."

"And not just your regular schoolwork. A monk will need to know many things beyond what a laborer's son would learn at school. You will need to know Latin. You will need to study theology. You will need to take learning and holiness very seriously. Are you prepared for this?"

"I am."

A thin smile crept across Grazio's lips. Francesco had a hard time reading him. He seemed happy but also pained.

"Then a monk you shall be," his father said.

Nothing further was said on the subject that evening, but it was on every heart and mind as Ave Marías and Pater Nosters drifted up to heaven from the Forgione home that autumn night.

CHAPTER 4

On the Threshold of Two Worlds

Francesco soon learned why his father had seemed pained by his desire to enter religious life. While Francesco was out retrieving the book, Grazio and Mamma Peppa had a brief discussion about the practical matters of Francesco entering the monastery. It was evident that the boy would need an education far beyond what the little school in Pietrelcina could offer him. His mother and father knew this meant hiring a private tutor. But money was tight, and Grazio would have to take on additional work to pay the expenses—most likely work that took him away from home.

As time marched on, the family continued to discuss Francesco's plans. His parents wondered if this was a phase he would soon outgrow. But it became clear that Francesco's desire was no mere passing fancy, no daydream of a boy's imagination. Francesco was entirely earnest about devoting his life to God as a religious.

Grazio's plan to raise the necessary money was to travel to the United States to work as a laborer, where wages were much higher than they were in Italy. Francesco was deeply moved by the sacrifice his father was willing to make for him and was even plagued by a sense of guilt. But he knew what God was calling him to do.

It took several months for Grazio to make the arrangements for his trip to America. By the time he departed, Francesco was nearly twelve. It was a bittersweet day. The entire family accompanied Grazio out of town to the crossing by the road that led to Benevento and then onward to Naples and the sea. It was a beautiful spring day, with a crisp blue sky and the white-petaled poppies bursting up across the countryside, occasionally punctuated by dazzling purple crocuses. Grazio and Mamma Peppa held Francesco's hands as they spoke about the future; Michele, now sixteen, carried little Grazia upon his shoulders; and Felicita and Pellegrina held hands and followed along behind, stopping occasionally to pick wildflowers from the roadside.

If only this walk could never end! Francesco thought. *If only we did not have to part!*

When they came to the crossroads, there were embraces and tearful goodbyes. Grazio hugged the girls, bidding them to be good and mind their mother. For Michele, a firm handshake and practical admonitions about the management of the fields and flock. When he came to Francesco, he tussled the boy's hair, then caressing his cheek, said, "Go with God, my boy. And say a prayer for your old papa as often as you can spare it." Francesco nodded as he blinked away tears. "Good boy," said Grazio, kissing Francesco upon the forehead.

"Well, go on before you miss your boat," said Mamma Peppa, embracing her husband tearfully. They had seldom been apart since the day of their wedding. Grazio pressed her to himself, peppering her cheek with kisses until her whimpering turned to laughter.

"Farewell, Forgiones! I shall write soon!" Then waving goodbye, he slung his sack over his shoulder, turned, and trotted off down the lane to Benevento. The family stood together, watching him from the crossroads until he disappeared, obscured by the hedges and clusters of birch that lined the road like an honor guard seeing Grazio off on his journey.

With the work on the farm and fields divided among his siblings, Francesco was ready to commit himself to full-time study. It would be some months until Papa's wages from America arrived and a tutor could be hired, so Mamma Peppa spent the time acquainting Francesco with the various monastic houses around Pietrelcina. Almost every village in the area had its own little monastery or convent.

"I want to be a Capuchin like Brother Camillo," Francesco told his mother.

Mamma Peppa accordingly made an appointment to take Francesco to the Capuchin friary of Morcone, seventeen miles northwest of Pietrelcina. Francesco harnessed Zio to the wagon, and he and his mother made the plodding three-hour trek to the Capuchin friary.

The town of Morcone spread out like a fan across a hillside, crowned at the top with an old castle, much like Pietrelcina. But the Capuchin friary was not in the town; rather, it rested in an isolated place outside Morcone, situated near a waterfall that came tumbling from the heights of Mount Mucre, the hill upon which Morcone stood. Francesco took an immediate liking to the place. It was ideal for a life of prayer.

Mamma Peppa and Francesco knocked at the old wooden door of the friary. To Francesco's joy, he was greeted by none other than Brother Camillo.

"Ah, Francesco! It's been too long!"

"Brother Camillo! It is so good to see you. My mother and I have come to see Father Tommaso. I intend to enter the Capuchins."

Brother Camillo grinned and extended his arms, hugging Francesco. "Bravo! Bravo! You have been faithful to the call of God and Saint Francis."

Father Tommaso was the novitiate master. It was his job to ascertain the preparation and authenticity of Francesco's vocation. This tall, slender man with penetrating eyes and a wrinkled brow and the characteristic bushy beard of the Capuchins met Francesco and his mother in the friary parlor. Scores of novices had passed under his scrutiny over the years.

After inquiring from Mamma Peppa about Francesco's family and upbringing, he asked to speak to the boy alone. Mamma Peppa bowed and slipped outside, and the two left inside took a seat.

"Francesco," Father Tommaso began, "I do not doubt the sincerity of your desire, but one of my jobs as novice master is to ensure you have a clear understanding of the sort of life you will have here at Morcone. Our Lord said, 'The spirit is willing, but the flesh is weak.' Despite your resolve, it is possible that you do not fully grasp what the Capuchin life means."

"Brother Camillo told me everything," Francesco replied.

"I do not doubt that he did, and he is an exemplary brother. But even Brother Camillo took a long time to adjust to life here. I would not be fulfilling my vocation if I did not scrutinize your resolve, especially given your young age."

"I understand," said Francesco.

Father Tommaso looked at Francesco out of the corner of his eye, his eyebrows furled in thought. Finally, he said, "Francesco, do you understand the friars' rooms are small and simple? You would sleep on a hard bed clothed in your habit."

"Even now I often sleep on the stone floor in my bedroom which I share with my brother."

"I see," Father Tommaso said, scratching at his beard. "The diet here is frugal and the food very plain. Would that not bore you? After all, boys like sweets and flavorful food."

"I do not care about such things," answered Francesco plainly.

Father Tommaso leaned in, his tone picking up intensity. "During the winter, the friary is as cold as ice. You must rise every night at midnight to join the friars for prayers. We take discipline three times per week"—here he produced a small scourge of knotted rope from the folds of his habit—"in reflection of how our Lord was scourged at his passion. Surely, this isn't the life you want for yourself?"

"I assure you, it is," replied Francesco.

"What do you think about Lent?" Father Tommaso asked.

"We keep our fasts strictly in our home."

Father Tommaso grinned. "That is good. But you should know—we keep *three* Lents here, and we fast every Friday of the year."

"This does not frighten me, Father. I want to do these things and be a good and holy monk."

Father Tommaso smiled. "You know, Francesco, your time will not be your own. You will be governed by our rule of life in all things. Every day at certain hours, you will assemble for prayers. And you will keep perpetual silence, save for short periods of recreation. When you are not praying, you will be studying the Rule, the liturgy, the Scriptures, and the lives of the saints. In all things, you will be expected to imitate them, especially our Seraphic Father Saint Francis."

Francesco looked at his feet in silence for some time, deep in thought.

"What do you have to say, Francesco? Does any of this give you pause?"

"No, Father Tommaso. This is the life I desire. This is why I want to enter Morcone. I am only sad I will have to wait some years to grow older before I am allowed."

Father Tommaso chuckled. "A good and pious soul you are." Then standing up, he said, "I have heard enough. I will recommend you to Father Superior. In the meantime, excel at your studies and continue the pious practices you have already begun. We will speak again."

Francesco dropped to his knees, seized Father Tommaso's hand, and kissed it in reverence. "Thank you, Father. I will! With all my heart, I promise I will!"

It was not until winter that Grazio's first package arrived from America, stuffed with several months' worth of wages and a letter bidding Francesco to study hard. Mamma Peppa inquired through the local schoolmaster and obtained a reference for a highly educated tutor, Don Domenico Tizzani. Tizzani was a renowned Latinist and experienced teacher. He called on the Forgiones shortly after the New Year to begin lessons with Francesco.

Tizzani was a lanky man with sunken cheeks and an air of haughtiness. He visited Francesco three times per week to tutor the boy in Latin and literature. Tizzani and Francesco spent many afternoons hunched over musty, old texts on the Forgione kitchen table, reviewing Latin drills and translating passages from Virgil and Horace.

Francesco enjoyed his lessons, but he struggled with Tizzani. The work he did with his tutor was far more challenging than what he did at the Pietrelcina school.

"Try it again, Francesco. *Pulvis et umbra sumus . . .*"

Francesco stared at the passage from Horace. "Ah . . . we are . . . we are . . ." he mumbled.

"We are *what*, Francesco? We are what?" insisted Tizzani.

"We are . . . a cushion, and . . ."

"A cushion! No, no! This is *pulvis*. Not *pulvinus*. Please, concentrate, Francesco!"

Tizzani rubbed his forehead—the boy was giving him a headache. Francesco sensed his teacher's frustration and grew more flustered. Tizzani had a reputation for being a skilled teacher, but Francesco thought little of the man. Though Francesco tried to love everyone, Tizzani's condescension and exacting manner tried the boy's patience. But there was something else about him as well. Something Francesco could not quite put his finger on.

"Francesco! Your answer?" barked Tizzani.

"I'm sorry, sir, I do not know."

Tizzani slammed his hand on the table. "*Dust and ash*! We are but dust and ash! *Porca vacca, accidenti!* Heavens above, do you even study at all, boy? Or are you just daft?"

Mamma Peppa stormed in. "What's going on in here? I heard a bang. Is Francesco behaving himself?"

"Signora Forgione, the boy is stubborn as a mule! We've reviewed this same passage for two weeks now, and he's scarcely made a lick of progress."

"I'm sorry to hear that. Should we increase his lessons? Perhaps four times a week? Of course, I will pay you more."

"All respect to you, Signora, but all the lire in Italy wouldn't make this boy a scholar."

"Surely, you are not saying Francesco cannot learn?" Mamma Peppa said indignantly.

"I am indeed," insisted Tizzani. "The boy is a *cretino*—*deficiente* in the brain!"

Mamma Peppa's eyes turned to fire. Francesco had seen this look many times. Tizzani was about to get it.

"Maybe it's *your* teaching that is *deficiente*!" she cried, waving her wooden ladle at the man. "The only *cretino* in the room is the one in the scholar's cap!"

Tizzani stood up and thumped his chest. "My reputation is well-attested all over Campania!"

As Francesco watched the two argue, something suddenly dawned on him. It was as if his mind were illumined with a beam of light that came to him from . . . *elsewhere*. He stood up.

"Master Tizzani, you are a priest."

Tizzani and Mamma Peppa stopped arguing and looked at him.

"What did you say, boy?" said Tizzani.

"You are a priest," he repeated.

"I most certainly am not! I am a married man! How dare you!"

"Francesco! Don't say such nonsense!" Mamma Peppa scolded.

"But he is, Mama," Francesco said calmly. "He was ordained in Naples. But he abandoned the priesthood to marry a woman. Isn't that true, Master Tizzani?"

Tizzani stepped back from the table, gasping in amazement. "How . . . how could you know that? Who told you?"

"I don't know," Francesco admitted. "I don't know how I know. But I know."

A solitary tear welled up in the corner of Tizzani's eye.

"Francesco!" his mother said. "Is this the reason you've been difficult with Master Tizzani?"

"I am sorry, but how can I prepare for the priesthood at the hands of a man who has abandoned it?"

The teacher grabbed his books and papers from the table. "I must go now!" He scrambled out the door as quickly as he could, leaving the wooden door open swinging on its hinges.

His mother looked at him in disbelief. "How did you know about that, Francesco?"

The boy shrugged. "Sometimes, I just know things."

In the days following, Mamma Peppa wrote to her husband about the affair with Domenico Tizzani. Papa sent a telegram back instructing her to find another tutor for the boy, one better suited to Francesco's sensibilities. Soon another instructor was found, and Francesco began to flourish in his studies. He caught up with his Latin. He read classic works of theology and spirituality. He grew in wisdom and in stature, and in favor with God and men.

After two and a half long years, Francesco was ready. It was January 6, 1903. Again, Mamma Peppa and Francesco stood before the doors of the friary at Morcone, this time ready to part ways forever. The boy had changed and grown, now head-to-head with her. Mamma was silent, wrapped in her shawl to protect against the crisp winter wind. Francesco, too, was quiet, standing on the threshold between two worlds. All that remained to pass from one to the other was to reach out and knock. But Francesco hesitated.

"You know, Mama, for a long time I feared this moment."

"Feared to leave us?"

"Yes. Feared that the pangs of separation would be too much. And I did suffer much. But last night, something happened to relieve me of that worry."

"Tell me, my son."

"Our Lord and Our Lady appeared to me in my dreams. Jesus placed his hand on my head and told me he had a plan for me and that I should not worry about anything. And ever since this morning, I have only felt peace."

Mamma Peppa was silent as a gust of wind blew a whisp of dusty snow across their feet.

"Perhaps you don't believe me?" Francesco asked.

"My boy, *mi amore*," said Mamma Peppa affectionately, stroking her son's head. "I've always believed you. Your love for God is so childlike. I remember the day I found you crying in the alley when you were eight. Do you remember? When the boys blasphemed after Mass. I felt bad and wanted to comfort you, but I also knew I couldn't give you what you needed. I knew your soul was more sensitive than mine and that the way you experience God's love is not something I can fully understand. But even so, I can always support you. And I always will."

She leaned forward and kissed her son on the forehead. Francesco closed his eyes, savoring the kiss as he embraced her. He remembered when he was a boy how imposing Mamma Peppa once seemed—how he could fling himself into her dress and be enfolded by her. Now, at age fourteen, he could wrap her entire wiry frame in his big arms. She seemed like a small woman.

He nuzzled his face into her shoulder. "Thank you, my holy mother, for everything you have done for me."

"Now you belong to me no more," she said. "You belong to God and to Saint Francis."

Francesco looked at his mother, smiling. He took her hand and pressed his lips to it in reverence, then without another word, he turned and knocked on the door of the friary.

CHAPTER 5

"This Is What I Was Made For"

Fifteen days after Francesco Forgione entered the friary at Morcone, he received the religious habit of a Capuchin and was given a new name—Fra Pio da Pietrelcina. The name Pio was in honor of Saint Pius I, the second-century martyr pope.

The day he shed his ordinary clothes to put on the brown Capuchin habit—January 22, 1903—Francesco recalled the words of Saint Paul in his letter to the Ephesians: "Put off your old man who is corrupted according to the desires of the flesh; be renewed in the spirit of your mind, and put on the new man created after the likeness of God in justice and holiness of truth." He was putting away his old way of living and literally putting on a new life, a new identity.

Mamma Peppa soon came to visit this new young man, Fra Pio, but the reunion was difficult. She'd hoped her son would smile and laugh with her, discuss his new life in the monastery, inquire about old acquaintances, and joyously receive some gifts she had brought. But Fra Pio was reserved, standing somberly, eyes cast down, arms folded with each hand buried in the opposite sleeve. He answered her many questions curtly, showing no interest in familiar conversation. The Master of Novices, Father Tommaso, led the confused and shaken woman out afterward.

"If I would have known he would act this way, I never would have come," she grumbled.

"Fra Pio is a novice beyond reproach," he told her. "Uncompromising and determined to be a saint. But I assure you, he loves you. During free time, he has spoken of the influence of his 'holy mother.' Even so, he is undergoing great changes right now, and you must give him time."

The woman took the priest's hand and kissed it. "'Everyone that has left house or brethren or sisters or father or mother or wife or children or lands for my name's sake shall receive a hundredfold and shall possess life everlasting,'" she said, quoting the Gospel. "Thank you for your reassurance, Padre."

"The best way you can aid him is with your prayers," said the Master of Novices. "God be with you."

Father Tommaso had spoken accurately of Fra Pio. The young novice took his total commitment to God with the utmost seriousness, allowing no room for half-measures in his observance of monastic discipline. He practiced self-denial, patience and threw himself into zealous prayer. Very soon, Fra Pio began to make great strides in the spiritual life.

It was not long after Mamma Peppa's visit that Grazio returned home from America. When his wife told him of their son's conduct, he became concerned.

"I want to see this for myself," he insisted. "I need to make sure he's not . . . unbalanced in the head or gone a little *pazzo*," he added, crossing his eyes and making a cuckoo gesture with his hand.

Grazio found his son as Mamma Peppa had reported but nonetheless went away content. When he returned home to the eager questions of his family, he shrugged and said, "I went all the way to America so the boy could become a monk. Well, I want him to be a *good* monk, and from what the Master of Novices tells me, Francesco—er, Pio—is on his way to being a saint. We should all be proud of him and support him with our prayers."

And so the family did, offering Rosaries for their Capuchin son every single night.

After a one-year novitiate, Fra Pio was permitted to make his temporary vows. On January 22, 1904, at the age of seventeen, Fra Pio knelt before the image of Our Lady of Grace in the chapel at Morcone. Surrounded by his brethren, he consecrated himself to God with the three vows of poverty, chastity, and obedience.

Now that he was officially a Capuchin, Fra Pio endeavored to become as holy as he could. One day while praying in the chapel before the statue of the Blessed Virgin, he noticed another friar, Fra Anastasio, praying the Rosary devoutly on his knees.

He's so holy, Fra Pio thought. *They say he prays twelve Rosaries a day.*

Pio was suddenly struck by an inspiration.

If Fra Anastasio can pray twelve a day, then I can pray fifteen a day!

From that day forward, Fra Pio devoted every spare moment to the recitation of the Holy Rosary. If he was not at table with the brothers or attending to the community prayers, he could be found in the choir alone, rosary beads dangling from his fingers as his lips moved in silent prayer.

The other brothers noticed Pio's extraordinary devotion. "He is praying fifteen Rosaries a day! That's more than Fra Anastasio!" they murmured.

Fra Anastasio soon heard about this, and before long, he, too, was appearing more frequently in the choir to say the Rosary.

"Fra Pio and Fra Anastasio are competing with each other!" the friars said in amusement.

Indeed, it was true—if Fra Anastasio was seen in the chapel praying his rosary, Fra Pio would follow suit. If Fra Pio saw Anastasio perched on the rocky crags on the slopes outside Morcone, beads in hand, then he, too, would immediately pray a Rosary. Though Fra Anastasio became irritated by the young friar's competition, monastic decorum prevented him from confronting Fra Pio about the obnoxious contest.

One night, a disturbance coming from a cell across the hall—which just so happened to be Fra Anastasio's room—woke Fra Pio up. It sounded as though his fellow brother was awake in the middle of the night, moving around.

He's still up praying the Rosary! Well, I won't let him beat me.

Pio clambered out of bed, took out his rosary, and began his prayers. But the noises coming from across the hall were . . . *strange*. They did not sound like an ordinary man moving about his room and praying. The sounds made the hair on Pio's neck stand up.

He quietly moved to the door of his cell and cracked it open, peering across the dark hall. A shuffle followed by a dull grunt came from the blackness.

"Brother Anastasio?" Pio whispered. "Are you all right? You haven't fallen asleep at your Rosaries, have you?"

Suddenly, two red eyes glowing like embers emerged from the darkness. Pio shrunk back as the eyes moved, following him. Pio began to discern the form of a black dog, large and hideous, crouching in the doorway.

Pio stumbled back into his room, making the sign of the cross and holding his rosary up as a shield. In a shaking voice that matched his shaking hands, he stammered, "*Ave María, grátia plena*!"

The demonic beast stared at him coolly for a moment as if unimpressed, then turned and bounded off down the hall. Pio scampered to the doorway and then to a window that was open at the end of the hallway. Pio ran to the open window. In the moonlight bathing Morcone, he watched as the black form darted over crags and rooftops before finally disappearing into the blackness of the night.

The next morning, Fra Pio went across the hall to ask Fra Anastasio if he had heard or seen anything strange in the night. But the room was empty. Pio told his superiors what

happened and inquired about Fra Anastasio. He discovered that Fra Anastasio had been moved to another room without him knowing it. The room across the hall had been empty.

After the troubling encounter, Fra Pio spent some time before the Blessed Sacrament in the monastery chapel. With his knuckles clutched in prayer, he pounded his head against his hands and wept.

I've been too proud. I should focus on my own shortcomings rather than outdoing somebody else.

The door to the chapel creaked open, breaking his concentration. Pio heard footsteps approach, and though his eyes remained closed, felt the presence of someone kneeling in the choir stall behind him.

"I heard what happened," came a voice over his shoulder. It was Fra Anastasio.

"I've been a fool," said Pio without turning around.

"We are all fools in the eyes of Our Lord."

Pio finally opened his eyes and turned around. He nodded and offered a small smile.

"Would you like to pray the Rosary . . . *together*?" Fra Anastasio asked.

"I would, Brother."

The two produced their beads and began to pray, the former competitors now joining their voices in unity to praise and petition the sweet Mother of Christ.

Pio was soon told that he would be studying for the priesthood. A Capuchin who is not yet a priest was known as "Fra," which means "brother." Upon becoming a priest, he would join the venerable ranks of the "padres." The young friar threw himself into his studies with his characteristic zeal. His entire life was consumed with prayer and study. Countless hours spent poring over books in his cell sharpened his mind, even as his rigorous prayer routine put callouses on his knees.

Weeks and months passed. Leaves turned autumn shades of bright before falling to the earth, and the snows came and blanketed the ground. When spring returned, the hillsides came back to life with verdant wildflowers and lush green grasses, thrilled to feel the sun again. The liturgical season of Lent passed with all its penances, followed by the joys of Eastertide. Through it all, Pio never faltered in his studies nor the observance of discipline; in fact, he intensified them. He read until his eyes burned, prayed until his fingers ached from being folded for hours, and fasted until his habit hung loose about his wiry frame.

One day at mealtime, the Superior noticed Fra Pio was acting strange. His responses to the prayers were lethargic, and he seemed uninterested in his food. He pulled Pio aside, noting his pale and clammy skin and the beads of sweat gathering on his forehead.

"Brother Pio, are you unwell?"

"I am very well, Father," answered Pio weakly, but it was clear something was amiss. His hands shook as he attempted to keep them hidden in the folds of his sleeves.

Father Superior felt his forehead. "You're burning up! Report to the infirmary immediately."

"Yes, Father."

Pio shuffled off to the infirmary, dragging his feet, and thus began his long battle with a mysterious illness that would plague him for years. It was difficult to say what ailed him. Some said he had worn himself out with his extreme disciplines; others said he had tuberculosis. Nobody could be sure. When Father Superior came to check on Pio the following day, he found him drenched in sweat and shaking from severe chills. When his condition did not improve for several weeks, Father Superior made the difficult decision to send Pio back to his family in Pietrelcina to recover his health.

Pio was upset at the news but submitted himself to the will of his superior. A few days later, he was loaded into the back of a wagon stuffed with hay, still feverish and shaking. Beside him lying on the hay was a little sack, carrying his books so he could continue with his studies. Father Superior and some of the brethren came to bid him farewell.

"Brother Pio," began the Superior, "you are being sent home to rest and recover, but remember our way of life. Keep the rule as best as you are able, given your condition. Use your free time to study. Honor the spirit of Saint Francis by your conduct. God willing, before long you will be returned to us and stand before the Lord as a priest."

Pio struggled to sit up and kiss the hand of his superior, then crossed himself for a blessing before collapsing back into the hay. Moments later, the wagon jolted, creaked, and began its slow, wobbling journey down the road toward home. Pio took a deep breath and looked up at the rich blue sky adorned with wispy clouds as he passed beneath it. The air was crisp and cool, refreshing in his nostrils. It felt good to be outside.

Every now and then, a bird came into view. Pio smiled and thought of the words of Christ.

Behold the birds of the air. They neither sow, nor do they reap nor gather into barns: and yet your heavenly Father feeds them. Are not you of much more value than they?

Pio folded his arms across his chest and closed his eyes, entrusting himself to the mercy of God. The gentle rocking of the cart and the occasional mumble—"*Costante lì, mulo*!"—from the peasant driver sent him into a sweet, untroubled sleep, the first he had in weeks.

Pio's sojourn from the monastic life would consume almost ten long years, punctuated by many adventures and trials. But Pio made the best of this difficult time, following his superior's advice. He deemed it best for his discipline if he did not stay in town with his family. Instead, he lived in an old, run-down farm building on his family's property in Piana Romana, in the fields he had worked with his father as a youth. The stone structure had not been inhabited for years, but his brother Michele brought down a bed, table, chairs, and some other necessities. Here, Pio could keep the rule of the friary, undisturbed. Mamma Peppa and Pio's siblings visited every few days to check on their Capuchin brother and bring him food. Thus, Pio settled into his long convalescence.

Many days, Pio was too ill to go out. He would lay in bed sweating and suffering from agonizing migraines, getting up only to vomit. Still other days, his illness seemed to vanish entirely, leaving Pio feeling strong and full of life. These days he would devote to study or to journeying into the countryside around Pietrelcina for prayer. He spent many afternoons praying the Breviary beneath the old elm tree where he had once studied as a boy. His favorite place for prayer, however, was atop a rocky eminence that jutted out from the hillside of Pietreclina. This steep limestone spur, known as the Morgione, could only be accessed by a steep ascent. Pio would climb up to the Morgione, digging his sandaled feet into the crags of the cliff and struggling to pull himself up with his weak arms. Perched atop the Morgione like an eagle in its nest, Pio possessed a commanding view of the entire valley. It was the perfect spot for spending hours in prayer.

Pio recovered his health enough to make his solemn profession on January 27, 1907, at the Church of Sant'Elia a Pianisi in Campobasso, some distance north of Pietrelcina. After this, his prayer life intensified even more, becoming fervent and passionate. His favorite subject for contemplation was Christ's passion. The thought of Jesus crucified often moved young Pio to tears.

Pio continued to divide his time between Pietrelcina and Morcone, returning to the monastery when his health permitted and going back home when his illness resurfaced. Gradually, dark hairs sprouted from his chin and grew into a fine black beard, the kind he had once admired on Brother Camillo. He passed imperceptibly from youth into manhood.

In 1909, Pio was ordained to the diaconate. Normally, many years would still need to elapse before his elevation to the priesthood, but because of his illness, he petitioned the Capuchins for early ordination. If he were to die unexpectedly, he wanted to die as a priest of God. His superiors agreed, and Pio was ordained on August 10, 1910, in the cathedral at Benevento. His mother, sisters, and brother all looked on with admiration as their beloved Francesco lay sprawled out on the floor in a cruciform posture, swathed in incense prepared for sacred ordination. Grazio was unfortunately absent, as he had returned to America again to provide for his family.

Archbishop Paolo Schinosi, facing the young Capuchin as he lay prostrate, prayed, "Hear us, we pray, O Lord God, and pour out on this servant of yours the blessing of the Holy Spirit and the power of priestly grace. And now as we present him for consecration in your benign presence, may you sustain them forever by the bounty of your gifts."

Pio arose and knelt before the archbishop, who placed his hands on Pio's head in the ancient and sacred gesture of ordination. After calling to mind the priestly exemplars of Aaron in the Old Testament, Archbishop Schinosi said, "Almighty Father, we pray that you bestow on this servant of yours the dignity of the priesthood. Renew in his heart the spirit of holiness, so that he may be steadfast in this second degree of the priestly office received from you, O God, and by his own life suggest a rule of life to others."

Pio's eyes were closed tightly, his brow furled in concentrated prayer, his hands folded in perfect symmetry. Mamma Peppa dabbed her eyes with a handkerchief as she watched the archbishop vest her son in the priestly chasuble, the characteristic vestment of the Catholic priesthood. After the ceremony ended, she ran up to her son.

"Father!" she said, dropping to her knees and kissing her son's hand. Pio smiled a tender, gentle smile and raised his right hand, making the sign of the cross and pronouncing his first priestly blessing, fittingly over his mother, who had formed him so much in the Faith and who now knelt before him as his spiritual daughter.

Even more surreal was Father Pio's first Mass, offered only four days later on the Vigil of the Assumption, at the altar of the Virgin Mother in Pietrelcina. The homily was delivered by Padre Agostino, Pio's theology instructor. Padre Agostino spoke of the graces of the Catholic priesthood, then turning to Father Pio, said, "Sadly, your health is not good, so it is unlikely you will become a preacher. My hopes for you are that you will become a great and conscientious confessor."

Pio had yet to hear any confessions and wondered what it would be like.

A great confessor? Who would go out of their way to confess to me?

Then came the Canon of the Mass and the consecration. Father Pio felt as though his heart would burst as he elevated the Sacred Host for the first time, gazing in awe at the marvel taking place in his hands—that Christ, the Second Person of the Blessed Trinity, should make Himself present as Pio pronounced the words of consecration.

"*Hoc est enim Corpus meum*," he said slowly and reverently, holding the Host aloft for the worship of the cosmos as the acolytes jingled the altar bells and the incense wafted up to heaven.

This is what I was made for, Pio thought.

That evening, when he was again alone in the little stone house in the Piana Romana, he opened his journal and jotted down the following prayer:

Oh Jesus, my heart's desire and my life, as I raise you up in trembling hands in the mystery of love, may I be with you, the way, the truth, and the life for the world, and for you a holy priest, a perfect victim.

Pio had no idea on that warm summer evening in 1910 how truly the Lord would answer this prayer.

CHAPTER 6

Wounds of Love

"Padre Pio!"

The young friar turned, still mouthing the prayers of the rosary dangling from his hand. A small girl ran toward him, up the cobblestone street of Pietrelcina.

"What can I do for you, *bambina*?"

"Please come to my house! My daddy is dying, and no one will come help him!"

"Why won't they help him?" asked Padre Pio.

"Please, just come!" the girl said, tugging on the friar's robes. With a flick of his wrist, Pio wrapped the rosary around his hand and followed the girl—though continuing to mutter Ave Marías the entire way.

She led him to a modest home up the street. Pio ducked his head beneath the threshold and entered. A sick, lanky man lay sprawled on a cot in the corner of a dimly lit den.

Padre Pio immediately understood why nobody would see the man.

Domenico Tizzani, Pio's former tutor, sat upright, sweating and shaking. "Forgione? Is that you?"

Padre Pio smiled, sitting down on the cot beside the man. "Ah, so you remember me, eh? I remember you, too. Maybe that is surprising, since as you said, I am *deficiente* in the brain."

A look of remorse came over Tizzani. "I'm sorry for the way I treated you, Padre."

Padre Pio waved his hand dismissively. "You were right. I still had much to learn."

Tizzani nodded gratefully, then in a raspy voice, said, "Nobody will come visit me because of my sins."

Padre Pio scratched at his beard thoughtfully. "Nobody wants to share the bedside of a disgraced priest. Whatever demon is coming for your soul, they want no part of it."

Tizzani winced. "Your bedside manner needs improving, Padre."

The priest shrugged. "Do you want the truth, or do you want platitudes? I'm telling it like it is. You abandoned the priesthood and broke your vows for a woman. Where is she now?"

"She died some years ago," replied Tizzani weakly.

Pio sat silently, fingering his rosary beads. "Well, I have some good news," he said finally. "The demon is not yet here. You still have time to repent."

"Will you give me Last Rites?"

"Are you sorry for your sins, Domenico Tizzani? Do you wish to be reconciled to God and his Church?"

"With all my heart," said Tizzani, a flame of passion enkindled in his eyes. "When I was young, I despised my priesthood. It seemed like an obstacle to keep me from the success I wanted in the world. Money. Esteem. Women. But now that I am here, on the cusp of death, all those things I chased seem like ashes. And I can feel the darkness enclosing about me. I can sense the mouth of the underworld waiting to swallow me up. Padre, I don't want to die this way. I want to be at peace. I want Christ."

"And Christ wants you," Pio said reassuringly. Then turning to Tizzani's daughter, "Little girl, please give your father and I a few moments alone while I hear his confession."

The girl nodded and stepped outside the small home.

Padre Pio emerged onto the street a few minutes later. "Go see your papa," he said to the girl. She smiled and ran inside, nearly knocking over Pio on her way through the door.

Tizzani had made a full confession, been given the sacrament of Extreme Unction, and received Viaticum—his last Holy Communion before crossing over to judgment. The sight was moving. Tizzani had wept, and Pio, too, shed a tear at the beauty of the reconciliation brought about by sincere remorse.

"A lost sheep returned to the fold," Pio said, taking his rosary back out to thank God. But his joy was thwarted by the sight of three dark figures leaning against a wall opposite Tizzani's house. Their clothes were shabby and stank like sulfur, their eyes malicious. A shadow fell over the street where they stood.

Sensing a sinister presence, Pio clutched his rosary tighter and made the sign of the cross. "What is your business?" he asked them.

"We're here for Tizzani," the figures said all at once. "He belongs to us."

Padre Pio scoffed. "Not anymore, he doesn't! I just heard his confession and gave him Holy Communion. You're going back to your master empty-handed today."

A collective *hiss* rose up from the three figures. It was as if they shared a common tongue. "We'll see you again, Pio!"

The sun slowly emerged from behind a cloud, pouring light over the street and pushing the figures away with the shadows. Pio walked away, vowing to double his prayers for Tizzani as he approached his last hour.

Though ordained a priest, Pio's mysterious illness prevented him from regular monastic life. His superiors decided it was best for him to continue living in Pietrelcina at the little farmhouse. But Pio was certainly not idle. He taught catechism to students in the Chiesa Sant'Anna parish, he provided religious direction to families and individuals, he baptized babies, married young lovers, blessed fields and farm equipment, buried the dearly departed, celebrated private Masses, and when he could, visited with his family.

He also heard confessions. *Everywhere.* In the parish confessional. On the street corner. Sitting under an elm tree in the Piana Romana. In private houses. Everywhere he went, he heard confessions. This did not stop Pio from feeling weak and inadequate as a confessor. It did not seem like he had any compelling insights or advice for his penitents; all he did was tell them whatever plain truth was before his face. Despite this, his reputation as a confessor spread far and wide. People loved his straightforward way of speaking. And—regardless of what Pio thought—his spiritual insights proved to be profound.

Pio always kept the words of his superior before his mind. *Remember our way of life. Keep the rule as best you are able, given your condition. Use your free time to study. Honor the spirit of Saint Francis by your conduct.* Padre Pio did his best to observe the Capuchin way of life in Pietrelcina. When his health permitted, he returned to Morcone to live among his fellow friars. And when he was away, he maintained constant communication with his superiors by letter.

Despite his busy schedule, Padre Pio always made time for prayer, either ascending the cliff to the Morgione or else sitting, legs folded, beneath the elm tree overlooking the field where he once tended his family's flock. The more he prayed, the more he wanted to pray. Prayer became entirely absorbing, such that he would lose track of time or not notice the approach of a storm. Sitting with his back against the elm, breviary in hand, he lifted his heart to God as he gazed out across the windswept fields around Pietrelcina. Prayer seemed like a doorway to another realm, a way he could sink into himself and find communion with the Lord.

One day in 1910, Pio was sitting beneath the elm tree, praying intensely, so focused that he was barely aware of his surroundings. The eyes of his mind dwelt on the Passion of Christ. The friar winced as he pictured the scourging of Christ. His brow began to drip with beads of sweat as he pondered the crown of thorns twisted upon the head of the suffering Lord. He heaved and sighed and cried out, "My Jesus!" as he imagined the nails being driven into the hands of Christ. Pio felt overwhelmed by the love with which Christ suffered on behalf of men. It seemed so vivid, so real.

In the midst of his reverie, he suddenly began to feel a burning sensation spreading across his palms. He opened his eyes and rubbed them. When the sensation grew stronger, he began to grimace. "Ah!" Then holding his hands up, he noticed a red spot, no bigger than a small coin, imprinted on the center of his palms. They were barely visible but tender to the touch and extremely painful. Pio leapt up and began to run toward his family's home but stumbled and fell. His feet too began to suffer from a sharp pain. He struggled to pull himself up and hobble toward his home, wincing like an injured soldier with every step.

An hour later, Pio came tumbling through the doorway of the Forgione home. His mother and sisters were working in the kitchen. Mamma Peppa glanced over her shoulder briefly but quickly returned to her cooking. "My son, I did not expect to see you here today. Will you be staying for dinner?"

When he did not respond, she turned around completely. Pio knelt on the floor, waving his hands in the air and rubbing them as if trying to cool them down from a burn.

"What is this nonsense?" she asked. "Are you a guitar player now?"

"Please, Mama, bring me a bowl of water!"

Mamma Peppa fetched her son a basin of water, though not as quickly as he would've liked. Pio sat down at the table and dunked his hands into the bowl. The water did little to relieve his pain.

"What's wrong with your hands? Let me see!"

"No, Mama, it's fine . . ."

"Let me see your hands," she repeated, jerking them out of the bowl. He grimaced as she examined his palms. Her eyes drifted back up to meet his. She shrugged. "I don't see anything."

Pio nodded, doing his best to hold back tears. "Yes, it's probably nothing, Mama. Don't worry about me."

The strange pain in Pio's hands marked the beginning of a long period of suffering for the friar. His hands and feet were in constant pain, despite there being no visible wounds. Sometimes the light red spots would reappear on his hands and feet, but they were barely noticeable. Pio was embarrassed and perplexed by the mysterious condition. He did not want to talk about it, fearing that others would say he had lost his mind.

Pio did feel obliged, however, to explain the entire affair to his spiritual director, Padre Agostino.

"My dear son," Padre Agostino replied, "the Lord has given you these wounds of love to help you identify with him in his suffering and to become a holy victim for the salvation of souls. Embrace whatever God gives you. As with all things, this is a grace."

Though Pio suffered greatly, his director was indeed correct—Pio discerned many graces that he received from his wounds. He noticed first and foremost that his prayer life adopted a greater intensity. Pio had always been spiritually sensitive, but now the spiritual world seemed to come alive even more. He became intuitively aware of peoples' spiritual struggles before they even told him, and he saw with greater clarity the battle being waged for their souls. Sometimes, he could even see his guardian angel or other mystical visions.

His Masses, too, began to change. It became difficult for Pio to pray the Canon of the Mass without getting overwhelmed at the majesty of what was occurring on the altar and in his very hands. Prayers like the Memento Domine and Hanc igitur, prayers that took most priests only a moment to say, took Pio many minutes to get through. Sometimes, after pronouncing the solemn words "*Hoc est enim Corpus meum* (This is My body)" and elevating the host, he would hold the Body of Christ aloft in silence for several minutes, gazing at the Host in adoration, tears welling in his eyes. Some parishioners began to complain.

"Why does he take so long? I have places to be!"

"I do not understand how a man could speak so slowly!"

"I think the tears he sheds are all an act."

Still, others were amazed and flocked to his Masses as if his being enraptured by the Blessed Sacrament was contagious and would spread to them. To watch Padre Pio offer Mass was to watch a man in love, and how could such love be restrained?

The graces that came to Pio were needed, as spiritual attacks against him increased in intensity as well. One night as he prayed before an image of the Sacred Heart in the little stone house at Piana Romana, he began to have trouble focusing. This was not normally a problem he encountered. But it was not internal confusion or doubts that distracted him; it was the frightening howls he could hear outside in the fields. Then came a *thud* banging against the wall or floor of the home.

Pio began to feel the presence of the evil one.

"Not tonight, Satan," he said dismissively. "You have no power here."

He continued his prayers, trying to block out the distractions and the growing darkness invading the room. Suddenly, a jar flew from the shelf and smashed against the floor! Pio opened his eyes and leapt up. Detestable creatures with horrible forms appeared in the room—long, twisted beasts with creeping legs and gangly looking figures with slender, grasping fingers, moving in to enclose Pio and devour him whole.

Padre Pio, however, was accustomed to the tricks of the demons and only laughed at them. "You must do better than that to separate me from my Lord!"

The demons howled in rage, hurling themselves upon Pio and swirling about him like a tornado. He was tossed to the floor so hard that the breath was knocked out of him. In the commotion, the pillow flew from his bed and exploded into a shower of feathers. Books opened—pages flipping by themselves—only to be flung across the room. The chairs at his little desk were slammed against the walls. Pio grunted as he felt the blow of invisible feet kicking him in the gut. The entire house erupted into demonic clatter, a chaotic racket out of which Pio could only discern the shrill blasphemies, cries, and filthy words uttered by the evil spirits.

Hunched in a ball, Pio closed his eyes and clamped his hands over his ears to block out the vile shrieks. "The Lord rebuke you, Satan!" he cried. He uttered prayers to Mary, Saint Michael, and his guardian angel. He invoked the name of Christ and the Holy Trinity and recited passages from the Psalms.

Finally, minutes later, the racket died down. All was quiet. Pio sat up and opened his eyes. The little farmhouse was wrecked. Every book, dish, and object had been thrown to the ground. Sheets were ripped off the bed. Table and chairs were overturned. And feathers from his exploded pillow blanketed the entire room. The only thing left untouched was the image of the Sacred Heart on the wall.

Pio gazed upon the flaming heart of Jesus and made the sign of the cross weakly. "*Deo gratias*," he whispered. The battered friar crawled up and propped his back against the cold stone wall of the house. He pulled up his habit, scanning the blue bruises that had already begun to appear on his legs and abdomen.

This would be only one of many such occurrences in Padre Pio's life. He wrote about these events to Padre Agostino, saying, "They beat me so brutally that I think it was a very great grace that I was able to stand it without dying." Having realized that Pio could not be persuaded to sin against God though temptation, the devil, in furious desperation, had turned to simply beating the poor friar.

Demons were not the only otherworldly visitors who intervened in Padre Pio's life. Not long after he received the first demonic beating, Padre Pio was saying daily Mass in Chiesa Sant'Anna in Pietrelcina. He had just offered the final blessing, and the parishioners were slowly filtering out of the little church. Padre Pio unvested and knelt in a front pew to make an act of thanksgiving as was his custom. He laid his head in his folded hands, closed his eyes, and prayed the prayer he had written on the day of his ordination: "Oh Jesus, my heart's desire and my life, as I raise you up in trembling hands in the mystery of love, may I be with you, the way, the truth, and the life for the world, and for you a holy priest, a perfect victim."

He remained there for some time, alone in the empty church. Then, suddenly, a great pain scorched his chest! He clutched at the burning sensation. "Ah!" If anyone had seen Pio, they might have assumed he was having a heart attack, but the reality was much more mystical. It felt as though a dart of fire had pierced his heart. The pain was so intense that he dabbed at his chest to see if he was bleeding. But there was no blood. He lurched over and collapsed into the pew, still grasping at his heart.

What is happening to me? Am I dying?

Then, looking up, Pio saw a strange figure standing over him, not malicious like the demons, but nonetheless it was clearly not of this world. In its hand, it held a flaming spear which it used to skewer Pio's heart. He shrieked each time the flaming blade entered him. It felt like his very soul was being sliced open and searched—scoured relentlessly by divine omnipotence, every tiny corner being gazed upon in a flaming light. Every thought, every feeling was exposed and laid bare before the withering light. Pio had never felt more pain, nor had he felt more insignificant, more inconsequential, more miniscule. In his agony, he moaned the words of Saint Francis: "Who am I . . . but thy servant . . . and a base worm?"

Then came the filling. The sensation of slicing and searching gradually changed. An intense heat began to well up inside him. Spiritually, it was as if he were being flooded with love for God, but physically it felt like his heart was expanding. He gasped for air like a drowning man. But in his desperation, he strangely felt peace. Pio could sense new depths of love he didn't even know were possible.

"Oh, my Jesus!" he called out, struggling to catch his breath. "My heart is going to burst!"

It was several hours later that two altar servers, Matteo and Sergio, came to the parish for vespers and discovered Padre Pio laying on the pew. The boys stood gazing down at the friar.

"Is he asleep?" Matteo asked.

"I don't think so," Sergio responded. "He's breathing very heavy. I don't think people breathe like that when they are sleeping."

Matteo's face lit up. "Hey, I've got an idea. Sergio."

He reached his finger out timidly and began tickling Pio under the nose. The boy snickered.

"Isn't it wrong to tickle a priest? It seems like . . ."

"Seems like what?"

"I don't know . . . a sin, I suppose."

"Pshhh, if anything, it's a work of charity!"

"How is it a work of charity to tickle a priest?"

"Well, he needs to be awake to say vespers in thirty minutes. You don't want him to be late for vespers, now do you? Or risk having people walk in here and see him sleeping?"

Sergio shrugged. It was hard to argue with that logic. The two boys leaned over Pio. Sergio kept tickling Pio's nose. The boys giggled as they watched the priest's nostrils flare at the agitation.

Pio twitched and itched at the sensation, then sat up rubbing his face. The boys ran to the sacristy, trying to contain their laughter.

Pio did not know how long he had been lying there. "It must almost be time for vespers!"

He lurched his body up onto his feet and stumbled toward the sacristy. His entire body felt warm and swollen and fatigued. But he also felt euphoric and light. He struggled to remember what had happened to him with the mysterious figure and the searing pain through his heart.

Was that a dream?

Through his chest, though not as intense as before, he felt warmth rising through his habit. He shut the sacristy door and approached a mirror. Trembling, Pio pulled his habit up over his head, the color draining from his face as he saw whisps of smoke rising off his flesh.

CHAPTER 7

Drowning in Glory

DESPITE HIS BEST efforts to devote himself to his religious vocation, Padre Pio soon found himself caught up in events that would change the world forever. In 1915, Italy entered World War I, fighting with the Allied Forces of Britain and France against the Austria-Hungarian, German, and Ottoman Empire. In November of that year, Padre Pio was called up for military service under an Italian law that allowed the government to draft citizens into the army. He was compelled to give up his monastic life and report for duty.

He was of course devastated by this turn of events. His one consolation was that, as a cleric, he was not required to serve in a combat unit. Rather, he was assigned to an army medical corps in Naples. Still, he cried bitterly the day he stripped himself of his Capuchin habit and donned the clothes of a commoner. His trip to the military encampment at Naples seemed like a hazy dream. Sitting in the back of a pickup truck with several other men, rucksack on his lap, Pio and the other recruits made the long, bumpy trek to Naples. The dark rainstorm that erupted in the sky on their journey, soaking the men to the bone, perfectly exemplified Pio's feelings.

One of the other men turned to Pio, speaking over the storm. "So, what do you do, *amico*? What's your story?"

"I'm a Capuchin priest," Pio responded.

"A priest! Ha!" the man snorted and began cursing and blaspheming. "A fine day your God has given us! You're a regular, Jonah. We should all toss you off the back of the truck right now."

The rest of the men laughed. For the remainder of the trip, Pio was referred to simply as "priest."

Enduring this sort of treatment and the other questionable behavior of the soldiers was a trial for Pio. He had always been sensitive to such things, but in military life it was impossible to escape it. Drunkenness, fighting, gossip, lewd conversation, blasphemy, and every sort of vice imaginable could be found in the barracks. It was like being trapped inside a filthy tavern. Pio was even forced to answer to *Francesco*, something he found difficult since he had abandoned that name years ago. He got himself into trouble more than once when commanding officers called "Francesco!" and he absentmindedly neglected to respond.

At night, Pio sat at the edge of his cot, reflecting on the last decade. He had been a solemnly professed Capuchin for nine years but had never been able to live a regular monastic life because of his illness. Now, his conscription into the war made returning to the monastery look even less likely. He buried his head in his hands and prayed in a whisper. "Oh God, why are you doing this to me?"

As always, God would answer this prayerful question by showing Pio that He had a plan. He would use his son to spread light in a time of darkness. Pio went on to receive medical training and learned how to tend to wounded soldiers. He consoled them in their agony, treating their physical injuries while ministering to their spirit. On a few occasions, he was able to hear the confessions of dying men and reconcile them with God before they passed beyond the veil of this life. These experiences engendered in him a deep compassion for the sick and dying. And even though he was at first teased by his fellow soldiers, they came to respect him, removing their hats when he walked by. No one spoke ill of him anymore.

But Pio's service would not last long. Ironically, the illness that kept him from Morcone also got him out of the army. One day, Pio was found writhing in his cot, drenched in sweat, and burning from fever. An army medic taking Pio's temperature was startled when the mercury shot out of the thermometer, shattering the glass.

"What do you make of this, *Tenente*?" the medic said to his commanding officer.

The lieutenant shook his head. "He's useless to us in this condition. Send him home to die."

Just like that, Padre Pio was thrown in the back of a wagon and carted back to Pietrelcina. It was a good thing, too. Around 700,000 Italians were killed in the war. Had Pio not been sent home, he very well could have been one of the many war casualties.

Pio's commander thought he was sending him home to die. But Pio did not die. He recovered and again took up the Capuchin habit. He was not long at Pietrelcina, however, for his superiors had commanded him to go to the friary at Foggia, a city in southern Italy, to work as a spiritual director. It seemed he had just arrived there when he was ordered to move again, this time reporting in the summer of 1916 to San Giovanni Rotondo, a mountainous town eighty miles south of Pietrelcina. Pio's superiors hoped the mountain air would be good for his health.

As he packed his few belongings yet again, he penned a quick letter to his mother:

I will be at San Giovanni Rotondo for a short time, for some relief and rest, to get a little mountain air.

Little did Pio know that his stay in San Giovanni Rotondo would be anything but a "short time."

The homes of San Giovanni Rotondo were scattered upon the slopes of Mount Gargano, little outposts of civilization in a rocky wilderness. Padre Pio's heart was filled with joy when he first entered the little town and took a deep breath of the fresh mountain air. Looking at the string of buildings that dotted the sides of Gargano, Pio made the sign of the cross and prayed, "Like broken bread, once dispersed over the hills, was brought together and became one loaf, so may thy Church be brought together from the ends of the earth into thy kingdom."

His first assignment in San Giovanni Rotondo was to work as a spiritual director to a group of boys at a junior seminary. Pio spent his days hearing confessions, offering spiritual talks, and offering guidance to those who suffered from youthful ignorance. It was good, wholesome work, and the boys took well to the eccentric friar. But all was not well, for Pio's old enemy would soon come calling.

One night, one of the seminary boys named Guido was suddenly awakened by a strange sound like that of metal being twisted or grinded. Guido sat up, straining his ears and wondering if it had only been his imagination, for now all he heard was silence, and his two roommates still snored away soundly. He had just returned his head to his pillow when a deep *thud* stirred him up again. Then came the sound of chains dragging on the floor. The strange noises made his hair stand up on his arms and legs. His roommates were now awake as well.

"What was that?" asked Gabriele.

"I believe it came from Padre Pio's room!" Guido whispered.

"Let's go check on him!" said the third boy, Lorenzo.

The three boys rose quickly from bed and carefully tiptoed down the dark hall toward Padre Pio's quarters. When they arrived at his door, they heard him moaning beyond it. "Oh, my Madonna!"

"He sounds hurt!" said Guido.

The boys burst through the door and peered into the darkness. The iron bar that supported the curtain around the bed had been torn and twisted, with bits of it scattered on the floor beside Pio, lying flat with blood trickling from his mouth.

"Padre!" the boys called. They rushed in to lift the friar from the ground.

"I'm fine, I'm fine," Pio wheezed. "Go back to bed."

"Padre, you're bleeding!" said Lorenzo.

Pio seemed surprised to hear this. He wiped at his lip and looked at the blood smeared on his finger. "Nonetheless, I am fine. Please, back to bed."

"Padre, what happened?" the boys demanded.

"I said go to bed! No more idle curiosity. Go!"

The boys scurried out of the room, their curiosity unquenched.

The following morning after chapel, as all the boys sat around the breakfast table, Guido, Lorenzo, and Gabriele could not help but share the bizarre story from the previous night. Some did not believe them, while those who did wanted to know more. But there was only so much the three boys could share since Padre Pio had kicked them out of his room.

Padre Pio suddenly entered the dining hall, quieting the boys' gossiping tongues. Though they tried to play coy, all eyes were on the priest, and Pio knew it. There was no hiding his swollen lip and blackened eye.

"Padre, what happened?" one of the braver boys blurted out.

"Yes, tell us!" called another, emboldened by the first boy.

Pio shook his head and made dismissive gestures with his hands, but the boys erupted into a chorus of questions.

"Silence!"

The boys fell quiet at the friar's booming command.

"Fine, I will tell you. Do you want to know why I received such a beating last night? Because I, your spiritual father, am willing to defend one of *you*."

The boys all looked at one another, confused. A few whispers passed between them.

Perceiving their thoughts, Pio continued. "I'll tell you what I mean. One of you was suffering a grave temptation against purity last night. He called out to the Blessed Mother, and I heard his cry. I got out of bed and began praying my rosary for him. I was successful. The attacks meant for that boy were directed at me instead. That boy slept peacefully through the night, while I went to battle for him."

The boys said nothing but continued to look around, wondering who it was. None of them wanted to confess that he was the one Pio spoke of, but every single one of them was in the chapel later that day, praying for protection against the snares and temptations of the evil one.

Days later, on a pleasant enough afternoon, Padre Pio led the boys on a hike up the slope of Gargano. The boys chatted away amongst themselves while Pio walked ahead, lost in contemplation, a rosary dangling from his hands.

Suddenly the priest stopped and clutched his heart! He fell down on a rock, wincing. The boys whispered among themselves, wondering what could be wrong. Still, they kept their distance. They had learned to give Padre Pio his space when he seemed to be having one of his "moments," as they called them.

A dark sadness fell over his face. He looked like he wanted to cry. Pio gestured for the children to gather round. The boys cautiously moved in, making a circle around the priest. Still holding his heart, Padre Pio said, "One of you has stabbed me, right in the heart!"

The boys looked at each other. "What do you mean, Padre?" one of them asked. "Who has stabbed you?"

Tears welled in his eyes and began to trickle down his stubbled cheeks. "Just this morning, one of you made a sacrilegious Holy Communion! And I was the very one who gave it to him. With these hands!"

The priest held his trembling hands up in front of his face as if in disgust that his own flesh had participated in the sacrilegious act. He bit his lip, trying to hold himself together. He felt the same as he had years ago, when he was a boy and heard the neighborhood children blaspheming in the street. But he could not hide behind a wooden gate and wait for his mother this time. Instead, he whispered a prayer to his spiritual mother. "Oh, Madonna, comfort my poor soul . . ."

Pio slowly rose to his feet. Wiping his nose on the sleeve of his habit, he said, "All right, then. Out with it. Time to confess."

One of the boys came forward in tears, dropping to his knees before Pio. "I was the one. Forgive me, Padre."

Pio's face lightened as a smile crossed his lips. "Stand up, son."

The boy obeyed. Padre Pio put his arm tenderly around the boy and escorted him some twenty feet away, allowing him to hear the boy's confession in private as the others waited behind.

Five minutes later, Pio pronounced the ancient formula of absolution, making the Sign of The Cross over the kneeling boy. "*Deínde ego te absólvo a peccátis tuis, in nómine Patris, et Fílii, et Spíritus Sancti.*"

The boy stood up, still sniffling. "I'm sorry, Padre."

Pio smiled and tussled the boy's hair. "I say to you, there is more rejoicing in heaven over one sinner who repents than of ninety-nine who need no repentance. Go, and sin no more."

The boy smiled and returned to his friends. Pio called out to the group. "All right, ten-minute rest and then we continue our hike!"

The boys scattered across the slope and sat down, eager to have some levity after such a heavy moment.

Pio wiped his sweaty brow and turned up toward the blue sky, closing his eyes. A crisp wind grazed his face and gave him peace. "Thank you, Lord," he said, stretching his arms into the air, standing in a cruciform posture. The peace of the moment was challenged by the pain he still felt in his chest. He massaged his sore breast muscle through his habit, but it did little to ease the pain. His palms and the soles of his feet ached as well. He looked at his hands—vaguely, almost imperceptibly, he could see a red spot on his palm.

He quickly closed his hands into fists and hid them away inside his sleeves. He called to the boys. "On second thought, let us pray a few minutes before we continue on."

"Yes, Padre!" the boys called in unison. They came running to the priest like sheep to the call of their shepherd. Padre Pio knelt on the path, leaning against the rock he had been sitting on. The boys, too, knelt devoutly wherever they were—on the path, on the rocks, spread throughout the rough mountain grass that carpeted the slope of Gargano. The boys' faces were serious, marked with a piety instilled in them from Pio's example. He smiled as he led them in prayer.

This was the kind of effect Padre Pio had on young men. Witnessing his own sufferings on their behalf, they were inspired to take their own spiritual lives more seriously, to lay hold of Christ and cling to him more ardently. In this way, Pio's sufferings became another expression of the truth Padre Agostino had shared with him after his experience beneath the elm tree back in 1910—Padre Pio was a holy victim for the salvation of souls. But the suffering Pio had always experienced on behalf of sinners his entire life was about to reach its culmination.

In September of 1918, the horrific slaughter of World War I was only a few weeks from ending.

Padre Pio was now thirty-one years old and had spent two years in San Giovanni Rotondo. His health had improved dramatically since his arrival there. The first wisps of gray had started to appear in his bushy black beard, signaling that his youth had been put behind him. He was pleased with his ministry to the boys, but he had further cause for joy—he had finally resumed regular monastic life at the Capuchin monastery in town, Our Lady of Grace. Life was good for Padre Pio.

After Mass one day, Pio retired to the monastery choir to pray and thank God for His goodness. He sat alone in the darkened room, kneeling in the choir stall where he had grown accustomed to praying the Divine Office with his brother Capuchins. The room was swathed in shadow, save for a tiny beam of sunlight that filtered in through the cracked door. Head in his hands, Pio wept tears of joy over finally being able to live the life he felt he was called to.

How good God is!

His heart felt aflame with love of God and man, whom God had suffered to redeem.

Use me, O Lord! Use me that all the world might acknowledge you!

His prayer soon trailed off into things too deep for words, pondering the sufferings of Christ for the sake of mankind. He felt entirely lost, sinking into the depths of the wounds of Christ.

Then, abruptly, a strange feeling came over Pio, one not of fear but of awe, the way a person might feel when confronted with something immeasurably bigger than oneself, like standing before the sea. He had a premonition that he should open his eyes.

Before him stood a strange figure that stole Pio's breath. The figure bore a striking resemblance to the mysterious stranger who had thrust a flaming spear through his heart in 1912 at Chiesa Sant'Anna. It was hard to capture the stranger's appearance; he seemed at once solid and ethereal, both clothed and unclothed, gloriously bright but easy, even pleasant, to look upon. The stranger's face was a mixture of love and power—but at the same time, Pio couldn't make out his features. It was as if this being existed beyond the confines of Pio's reality.

Pio looked at the stranger's feet. Pools of blood were forming on the stone floor of the choir all around him. Then the figure held his arms aloft. His hands, too, were dripping blood. Pio gasped as light radiated from the stranger, seeming to dissolve their surroundings—the walls, the floor, the very existence of the choir seemed weak and indeterminate compared to the power of the stranger. The air felt thick like water. It seemed as though Pio was drowning in a glory too great for his pathetic human frame to endure.

He grasped his heart, feeling the familiar pain as though it was about to burst from his chest. "Lord, save me!" The whole room seemed to be scrambled, hazy. Pio could no longer see the stranger, nor even his own hand before his face. He cried repeatedly, "Lord, save me!" He was sure he was dying.

Then suddenly, the man was gone. The choir was back to normal. The narrow slit of sunlight beaming in through a crack in the door splashed on the dark stone floor. Pio could hear nothing but the sound of his own breathing.

He leaned back in his choir stall and took a deep breath, thankful the strange episode seemed to be over. But a sharp, shooting pain still flashed across his body. He groaned and looked down. Blood stained the side of his habit. He pressed his hand to his side and felt a hot sensation. He looked at his hand. Blood, not just wiped there from his side, but oozing out of his very palm as well.

"No . . ." he groaned in a panic. "No, please!"

He looked at his other hand. It, too, was bleeding profusely from the palm. Pio tried to stand up but fell upon

the floor, his aching feet unable to support him. He looked down. They, too, were covered in blood.

Pio crawled across the floor of the choir before collapsing in exhaustion in front of the door. The little beam of sunlight was still shining through the crack, creating a solitary point of illumination in the darkened room. Pio reached his hand up into the light, terrified when he saw the beam flowing through a hole in his pierced palm.

CHAPTER 8

Poked, Prodded, and Gawked At

PADRE PIO SAT in a wooden chair, his eyes downcast, hands folded into the sleeves of his habit. Around him stood a host of men—spiritual advisers, his monastic superiors, local doctors, and the Provincial Superior of the Capuchin Order.

Dr. Luigi Romanelli paced about the room, reviewing his notes. "Look, I've told you already, the wounds are not superficial. They are substantial. When you put your thumb on his palm and index finger on the back and apply pressure, you can tell there is a void. This isn't a scratch or a cut. Pio has holes straight through his hands."

"I disagree," replied Dr. Amico Bignami. "It's probably a type of skin necrosis that Padre Pio keeps from healing by applying chemicals to it."

"Necrosis? Chemicals?" exclaimed Dr. Romanelli. "Are we seeing the same thing? There's no inflammation around the wound that would suggest the use of any chemical. I've never heard of necrosis making holes straight through a hand!"

"Well, there must be some scientific explanation!" demanded Dr. Bignami.

Father Serelli, Pio's superior at Our Lady of Grace, was losing patience with the whole charade. He turned to Pio. "Padre, tell us again what happened."

"He's already told us dozens of times over the past nine months!" interjected Padre Benedetto, Padre Pio's confessor and spiritual director. "What more do you want from him?"

"You're the one responsible for this!" another brother interjected. It was Padre Giovanni, assistant to the Provincial Superior. "It's clear what's going on here! Pio is a simpleton whom you and that crank Padre Agostino have been taking advantage of, filling his head with all sorts of nonsense about visions and ecstasies and making this village idiot think he's a saint!"

"I never claimed to be a saint," Pio said softly.

Padre Benedetto jumped to his defense. "Pio is not a village idiot! You are obviously not qualified to judge things you know nothing about, Padre."

The room erupted into a cacophony of disagreement and accusation.

"Calm yourselves, brethren," said Padre Angelo, the Provincial Superior of the Capuchins in Apulia. "This rancor is hardly befitting for disciples of Saint Francis."

The men calmed themselves. Padre Angelo paced across the room, hand on his chin. Pio's head remained drooped toward the floor.

"I think we can all agree that Pio's wounds are real. They are not a product of an overactive imagination. How they came to be is another question, but we can all see they are real and substantial."

The men all nodded in agreement.

"The problem we have is not Pio's wounds," said Father Serelli. "It is out there."

The priest gestured outside where a crowd of people had gathered at the front of the monastery: people leaving letters for Pio at the front door, women calling out prayer requests, the sick and injured asking to see Pio, elderly women praying the Rosary.

"It's not too much of a crowd," said Padre Benedetto, shrugging. "What do you want Pio to do about it? He didn't ask for this. He has kept his wounds to himself."

"Oh please, don't be naïve, Padre!" snorted Padre Giovanni. "People were gossiping about this all the way in Benevento a week after it happened. How do you think that gossip started? And the way Pio wears those . . . those fingerless gloves everywhere—he might as well just paint a sign that says, 'Look at me!'"

"I'm only saying that we need to handle this properly," said Father Serelli. "Every day, someone comes here asking to speak with him. The letters continue to pour in. I am afraid it is becoming a disturbance. What do you think, Padre Angelo?"

The old friar ran his fingers through his grizzled beard. After a moment, he spoke softly. "We will continue to investigate Pio's wounds. I feel I must seek the judgment of the Holy See on this matter. In the meantime, Padre Pio, you are absolutely forbidden from showing your wounds to anybody or speaking of them, except to your spiritual director. And no visitors are to see Pio, save for family. Do you understand, Pio?"

"Yes, Father Superior."

The men began to file out of the room, the two doctors still locked in their dispute. Padre Benedetto placed his hands on Pio's shoulders. "Don't worry, brother. This will all be sorted out quickly."

Unbeknownst to Padre Benedetto, Pio's troubles were only beginning.

Many other doctors came to study the wounds of Padre Pio. They were being referred to as the "stigmata," the sacred wounds of Christ impressed upon his flesh as a sign of his likeness to Jesus. Pio, of course, did not refer to them that way; he did not refer to them at all, faithful as he was to the directive of his superiors. But as hard as he tried, they were difficult to conceal. The wounds in his feet were sometimes better, sometimes worse. The wounds in his hands, however, bled frequently and needed to be wrapped in gauze and hidden with gloves. The wound on his side was shaped like a little cross. It oozed blood continually and needed to be bandaged daily.

One day in 1920, there came a knock at the friary door. A tall, broad-shouldered Franciscan with a thick chin and dark, beady eyes greeted the friars with a bow. "I am Father Agostino Gemelli, a physician. I have been sent by the Holy See to examine the wounds of Padre Pio."

A great commotion ensued. "Pio's case has finally reached the ears of the Holy Father!" the friars said. Gemelli was kept waiting in the parlor while Father Serelli and Padre Pio were sent for. When Pio entered the parlor, Gemelli sized him up with a look of incredulity. Pio merely bowed and took a seat.

"Padre Gemelli, we are honored by your presence," began Father Serelli. "To what do we owe the honor?"

"I have come on the request of the Holy See to examine the wounds of Padre Pio," said Gemelli curtly. "News of Pio's . . . situation . . . has been brought to the Holy Father, and I have been sent to look into the matter."

Padre Pio looked at the man. "Could you please show me the directive from the Holy See?"

Gemelli chuckled uncomfortably. "Directive? I was sent personally by the Cardinal Secretary of State Merry del Val himself! I come on the highest authority!"

"If it is as you say, Padre Gemelli, then surely you have some proof of this," said Father Serelli calmly. "It is common courtesy for those sent from the Holy See to bear some letter of authorization."

"Proof? I am a very distinguished physician! Isn't my word enough? I've come all the way from Rome!"

Pio stood up. "Padre Gemelli, I have been examined, poked, prodded, and gawked at more times than you can imagine. Though this has been a cross, I am a religious and will submit in holy obedience to my superiors. All I ask is that you prove you are someone I must submit to."

"Insolence! Disobedience!" Padre Gemelli exclaimed.

"Disobedience to whom?" Father Serelli said. "You are not Padre Pio's superior. I am."

"I cannot believe you would encourage this arrogance, Father Serelli!"

"We do not mean to be obstinate, Padre Gemelli. But you must understand our situation. Regrettably, Padre Pio has become a great curiosity. Every day, people come here asking to see his wounds. Sometimes, they resort to quite inventive deceptions. Last month, we had a man pretending to be a priest saying he came from the archbishop's chancery. Even doctors try to come under false pretenses, saying they are sent from the government, but they are truly here only to satisfy their own curiosity. Anyone who wants to examine Pio's wounds needs written authorization, and that includes visitors from the Holy See. If you come on behalf of the Cardinal Secretary of State, it should not be difficult for you to obtain the proper credentials."

Padre Gemelli's face flared red. "I've never been so insulted in all my life! You haven't heard the last of me!" He rose quickly from his chair and left the room, slamming the door behind him.

Pio immediately knelt upon the floor, took Father Serelli's hands into his own gloved palms, and pressed them to his forehead. "Padre, thank you for defending me, but I am sorry I have caused you so much trouble! I am nothing but a burden to you!"

"Get up, son," said Father Serelli, lifting Pio from his knees. "It is true, you have indeed made my life more . . . eh, *complicated*. I do not know what to make of all this. But you are my spiritual son, and I will protect you."

Despite Father Serelli's support and protection, Agostino Gemelli was, in fact, sent by the Holy See. He returned to Rome enraged and wrote a fuming letter about Pio:

> *Padre Pio is a man of restricted field of knowledge, low mental energy, monotonous ideas, little volition. If he sometimes appears humble, it is more out of mental deficiency than any virtue. Padre Pio is a poor, sick man of little intelligence being used by his superiors to promote a fraud.*

Though at first nothing came of the letter, copies of it began circulating throughout the upper crust of the Italian Church hierarchy. Some, skeptical of Gemelli's report, sent their own doctors to examine Pio. Others were convinced by Gemelli and believed Pio was a fraud. Every Italian clergyman of importance seemed to have his own opinion on Padre Pio. One man who read Gemelli's letter with great interest was Cardinal Achille Ratti, the Archbishop of Milan. *This Pio fellow sounds like bad news*, he thought. A few months later, this Archbishop Achille Ratti was elected Pope Pius XI.

In the meantime, Pio's fame had only increased. May 31, 1923, was a typical day for the now-famous friar of San Giovanni Rotondo. It was mid-morning, and Pio had just finished celebrating Mass. As he had grown accustomed to doing at this point in the day, he sat in his cell poring through letters piled before him like a small mountain upon his desk. Most of them were from strangers requesting prayers or advice.

So many letters had come for Padre Pio that his superiors assigned him an assistant to help him respond to them all, a novice named Fra Christoforo. Christoforo pulled a letter from the pile and opened it. "This letter is from a lady named Marianna in Palermo. She says . . . eh . . . let's see . . ." Christoforo scanned the lengthy correspondence, trying to get the gist of the request. "Well, eh, she wants prayers and spiritual advice. She goes to Mass three times a week and prays irregularly. She wants to know how she can become holier. Then there's, eh, three or four pages more she wrote about her life and spiritual struggles."

Pio sighed and shook his head. He took pen to paper and began scribbling. Then handing the paper to Fra Christoforo, said, "Send this to Lady Marianna." Christoforo was surprised Pio responded to such a lengthy letter so quickly. He read Pio's response:

Dear Madame,

If you want to be holier, do the things to make it so. Go to Mass seven days a week instead of three, and pray regularly instead of irregularly.

In Christ under Mary,
Padre Pio of San Giovanni Rotondo

Christoforo chuckled at the simplicity and wisdom of Pio's response. "What?" Pio said with a twinkle in his eye. "Holiness really isn't that complicated. The answer is usually right in front of you. So, how many is that so far?"

"That was ten this morning so far, Padre."

"Very good. Next?"

Christoforo opened another letter. "A tradesmen of Lazio requests prayers for the healing of his daughter, Benedicta. She is ill with consumption."

Pio nodded, "Ah, tuberculosis is a terrible affliction. I shall pray for her," he said, and jotted the name BENEDICTA in a ledger he kept near him to organize prayer requests he received. "Next?"

"Let's see . . . hmm . . . this one is from a farmer's wife named Catherina. Her son Giuseppe has gone missing. She is terribly frightened for him and prays for his safe return."

Pio nodded and began scribbling a response. "The boy is not missing," he said while he wrote. "He took off to the city with his dissolute friends. He will be back soon. And he will need a whipping, if you ask me."

Pio handed the note to Christoforo.

"How could you possibly know that, Padre?" Christoforo asked.

Pio looked at the young novice with a withering glare. Christoforo blushed and mumbled apologies. Seeing the novice's discomfort, Pio's glare turned to a wry smile. "My guardian angel told me," he said, winking. "But come now, we've many more to get through! Your job is not to ask questions but to help me with these letters!"

"Yes, Padre. I'm sorry," said Christoforo.

Just then, another friar entered Pio's cell. "A letter for you, Padre Pio."

"What else is new?" joked Pio, gesturing to the mound of letters upon his desk.

"This one is from the Holy See."

Pio's eyes piqued with alarm. "Let me see."

He took the letter, opened it, and read it carefully. His countenance sank as he read it.

"What is it, Padre?" asked Christoforo.

"The Holy Office believes I am dangerous," Pio replied weakly. "The new Holy Father is against me. They are isolating me."

"Isolating you? How?"

"I may no longer say Masses publicly. I can celebrate Mass only in the friary chapel here at Our Lady of Grace—and with no one attending. And I may not respond to any letters."

A few moments later, two more brothers arrived in Pio's cell with a large sack. "Father Superior has ordered us to collect all these letters, Padre."

"Of course," said Pio, waving his hand.

The brothers gathered every letter into the sack. Pio's desk was empty for the first time in over a year. Before departing, one of the friars said, "Oh, Fra Christoforo, you will no longer be working with Padre Pio either. Please return to your cell."

Christoforo bowed and left, leaving Pio alone in his cell.

Pio dealt with his isolation as best he could. Thankfully, he was not left entirely alone. Though he could no longer work with children or offer spiritual direction, he still participated in prayers with his brothers, he could still hear confessions, and he occasionally went on errands into town for Father Superior. He was essentially a priest without a ministry, which greatly grieved Padre Pio. He bore his trial with patience, however, offering Mass privately every day and praying for his superiors and the Holy Father. He asked for God to use this trial to strengthen his faith.

Even though he was no longer answering letters, he was still praying for the people who had reached out to him. Gradually, over the remainder of 1923, word began filtering back to San Giovanni Rotondo that Pio's prayers were being answered. People were even claiming miracles through Padre Pio's intercession. Conversions. Healings. Favors granted. All manner of things were being attributed to Pio. People all over Italy spoke excitedly about "the saint of San Giovanni Rotondo."

Pio himself was unaware of this, as his superiors intercepted all his mail and were careful not to tell him about these things. He continued his prayers and private Masses in ignorance, oblivious of his growing renown—that is, until the following summer when the Holy Office again issued a decree against Padre Pio. This second decree reaffirmed the letter of 1923, with the added observation that there was no evidence that Pio had worked any miracles and that neither Pio nor his superiors should in any way suggest otherwise.

Pio was shocked to learn of this second decree, since he had no idea people were claiming miracles through his intercession. When asked about it, he shrugged, "It is God who worked these wonders, not me. The beauty in a sculpture is due to the skill of the sculptor, not the hammer and chisel he wields. If God has used me as his hammer and chisel, it is to him that thanks are due. I have done nothing."

Not long after this, Agostino Gemelli returned to San Giovanni Rotondo. Again, he met with Padre Pio and Father

Serelli. He handed Father Serelli an envelope. "Inside, you will find my explicit authorization from the Holy See to carry out a full medical examination on Padre Pio and write a report for the Holy Office."

Father Serelli flipped through the documents. "This is all in order. Padre Pio, you will submit to examination by Padre Gemelli. You will show him whatever he wishes to see and answer all his questions."

"Yes, Padre."

As could be expected, Gemelli's examination was critical of Pio. Gemelli's final report to the Holy Office accused Padre Pio of faking his wounds. He wrote:

These wounds are clearly self-inflicted. They appear to have been caused by a corrosive chemical that Padre Pio must be applying to them to keep them fresh.

This report to Rome ensured that Pio would remain isolated for the foreseeable future.

The accusations that Pio was faking his stigmata were hurtful to him. Things were made even more difficult by the fact that he could not form a response or defend himself. The friary, the town, and the entire region were abuzz with gossip about the famous friar, yet he was forbidden to speak about the matter.

Pio offered his sufferings up to God. "Oh Lord, use my poor sufferings for the salvation of sinners," he prayed fervently as he offered Mass alone in the friary chapel, beating his head against the altar while he knelt at the consecration. "Unworthy though I am, use me as Your instrument to bring souls to You."

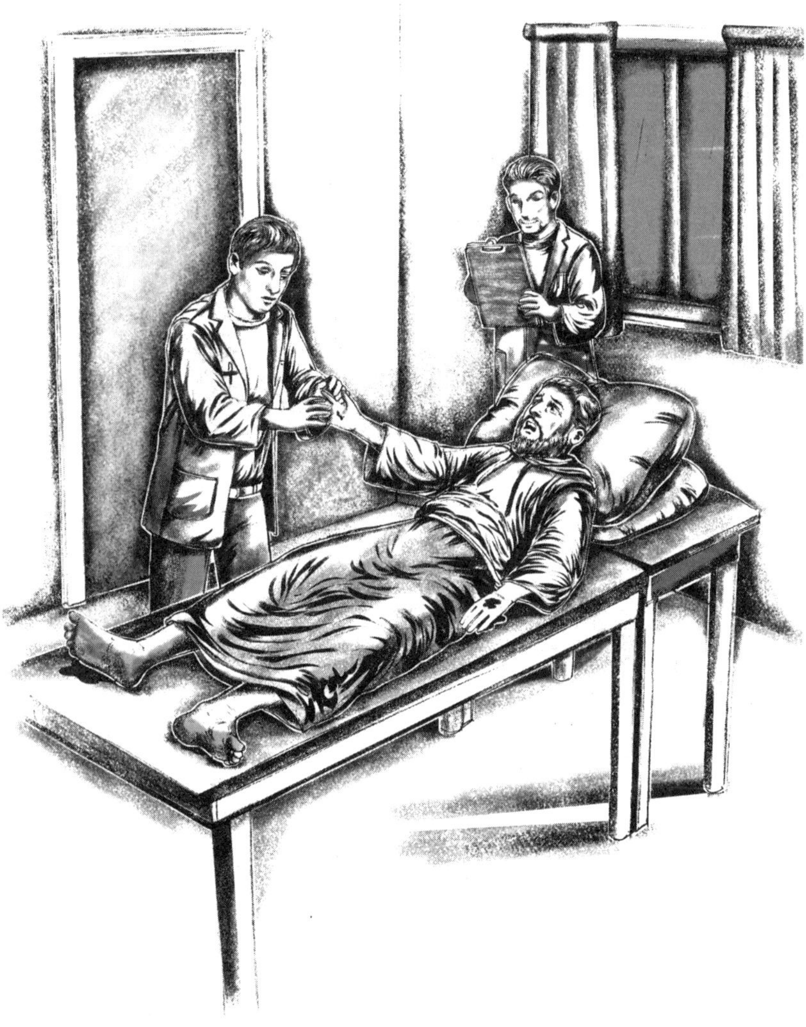

In 1925, Padre Pio became ill again. His abdomen was in constant pain. Doctors determined that Pio had suffered a hernia. He would need to have surgery. Due to all the excitement about Pio's stigmata, his superiors decided it would be best if the surgery could be carried out within the friary. Thus, his cell was converted into a makeshift hospital room.

The surgery was to be carried out by Dr. Giorgio Festa, a local doctor who had once examined Pio's wounds back in 1919 and believed them to be authentic. On the day of the operation, Dr. Festa was admitted to the friary along with his medical attendants. Pio was sitting on his bed-turned-operating table, clothed in a white surgical gown, his brown habit draped over a chair.

Dr. Festa brought over a stand with two tanks fixed to it. "This is the ethylene gas, Padre," he said. "It's anesthesia. These tanks will be connected to a tube that runs to a mask we will put over your mouth and nose. When we begin the procedure, you can just rest and breathe normally. The ethylene will have you unconscious in a few minutes."

"No anesthesia," said Pio dismissively.

Dr. Festa blinked in disbelief. "Padre, there's no need to try to be heroic here. No one will think less of you if you use anesthesia."

Pio chuckled. "You think this is about my ego, doctor?"

"Well, what is it?"

"I am under strict orders from my superior that no one is allowed to see my wounds. If I let you knock me unconscious, you will not be able to restrain your curiosity. You and your assistants will look at my wounds. I would rather stay awake and suffer the surgery fully conscious than permit that."

Festa looked grieved. "Padre, for heaven's sake, I'm going to cut your stomach open and stuff your intestine back into its lining by hand!" He held out the anesthetic mask. "Please, for the love of God, take the anesthesia. I promise I won't look at your wounds!"

"No anesthesia," Pio repeated.

The doctor threw the mask down. "Your stubbornness will be the death of you!"

"Mother could not make me sweeter, nor could she make me more stubborn," Pio wisecracked as he lied back on the operating table.

The operation was carried out without Pio receiving any pain medication. He bore his suffering in stoic silence while Dr. Festa sliced open his stomach with a scalpel. He stared up at the ceiling with icy resignation, teeth clenched while Festa's attendants held the incision open so the doctor could work on the herniated intestine.

But the operation proved too overwhelming even for Pio's resolve. The friar finally fainted from the pain. Once Dr. Festa had finished repairing the hernia, he glanced toward Pio's face. He was still unconscious. The doctor slid his eyes down to Pio's hands.

One little look won't hurt anyone.

He removed Pio's gloves and examined the stigmata wounds with his attendants.

"Extraordinary! They're just as fresh as they were when I first saw them seven years ago."

"What is that smell, doctor?" asked one of the attendants.

"Isn't it lovely?" said Dr. Festa. "I noticed that years ago as well. His wounds have a fragrance about them, almost like . . . perfume, or flowers. I think this man is a saint."

Pio was subsequently stitched up, and sometime later gradually resumed consciousness.

"Ah, my patient is waking up! How are you feeling, Padre?" Dr. Festa asked, leaning over Pio.

Pio opened his eyes weakly. "Doctor," he wheezed through parched lips, "I know what you did. You betrayed me."

CHAPTER 9

Mammella!

Flavio and Stefano stood in the line, growing more impatient by the minute. The crowd of penitents waiting before Padre Pio's little wooden confessional stretched into the narthex and out onto the front steps of San Giovanni Rotondo. The two men stood just inside the church doors, some thirty people still in front of them.

"I knew there would be a lot of people, but I didn't expect *this* many!" fumed Flavio.

"Isn't it amazing how many ignorant fools still get taken in by this superstition?" asked Stefano.

"Don't worry about that. We're going to expose this fellow for the fraud he is!"

The two men smiled deviously. Around them, pious men and women stood in line, praying their rosaries.

Fortunately, the line moved quickly. Padre Pio had a reputation as an excellent confessor but an expeditious one. His confessions seldom lasted longer than two minutes, and he was famously curt with people who rambled or made excuses for their sins. It was not long before the two men's turn drew near.

"So, what fake sin are you going to confess?" smirked Flavio.

Stefano grinned. "Oh, let's see . . . ah, I know! I'm going to tell him I'm a notorious bank robber who has stolen millions and killed many people!"

Flavio chuckled. "I think I will be a little more subtle, confess things that any person would confess. A little lying here, a little cursing there. Maybe some lust? Ha! I want him to really think this is real."

It was Stefano's turn. He ducked into the confessional, winking at Flavio as he shut the door behind him. Flavio stood next in line grinning, barely able to contain his excitement over exposing this silly ritual.

Five minutes later, Stefano had still not left the confessional, nor could any noise be heard from inside. Flavio began to shift about uncomfortably. Was something wrong? The women in line behind him continued to thumb their rosary beads. *"Ave María, grátia plena, Dóminus tecum . . ."* one began, then the crowd of penitents would intone, *"Santca María, Mater Dei, ora pro nobis peccatoribus, nunc et in hora mortis nostræ. Amen,"* in a droning response.

Finally, the confessional door burst open, and Stefano came lunging out. He stared at Flavio, eyes red, agitated.

"Stefano, what happened? Come here, let me talk to you."

Stefano waved his friend away with a swipe of his hand and clambered out the narthex of the church into the street. Flavio stood still, dumbfounded.

"Sir, it's your turn!" the woman behind him said, gently pushing Flavio forward.

"Oh, yes, apologies," he said awkwardly. He walked inside and shut the door.

The confessional was a small wooden chamber, scarcely large enough for a grown man to fit on the kneeler. With the door closed, it left Flavio swathed in total darkness.

What in the world happened to Stefano in here?

There was a sliding noise, and suddenly the confessional grille was exposed—the intricately wrought screen that allowed the penitent to speak to the priest on the other side. Flavio squinted to get a glimpse of the mysterious man beyond the grille. But the screen obscured the priest's face, while the darkness did the rest. All Flavio could make out was a rough outline of a bearded man.

"Well . . . ?" the priest said from behind the screen.

"Oh! Um, yes!" Flavio had not been to confession in years, and it took him a moment to remember the protocol. "Bless me, Father, for I have sinned . . ."

"You do not believe that," the priest said curtly.

Flavio froze. "What do you mean, Padre? I've come to confess—"

"—I know what you are up to. You and that friend of yours. I know you are Freemasons, atheists, and that you've come to mock me and commit sacrilege against this sacrament."

Flavio bit his lip in anger.

Stefano! That idiot told him our plan!

"Your friend told me nothing more than you have," Pio said as if reading Flavio's thoughts. "And I will tell you what I told him—you think this is a joke, a game? Your immortal soul is at stake. Why throw it all away? God is calling you to repentance. Clean up your life. Stop associating with atheists. And good heavens, stop going to that tavern on Friday nights and consorting with that woman! Get your drinking under control."

Flavio began to shake. How did he know about the tavern? The woman? The drinking? "Padre . . . I . . . I—"

"—am going to come back next week and make a sincere confession," Pio said, finishing the man's sentence.

"Yes, Padre!" Flavio said, his lip quivering, his insides feeling like jelly. "I will."

"Good. Now, get out of here and send the next penitent in."

Flavio turned and lunged out of the confessional, just as Stefano had done. He began to cry as he stumbled out of the church and looked for his friend. Flavio and Stefano would both return to Padre Pio and make general confessions, reconciling with the Church.

But that would occur next week. For now, Pio sat in the confessional hearing more confessions for another hour, listening to penitent after penitent unburden their consciences to him. He was sometimes harsh, sometimes gentle, depending on the disposition of the penitent. Pio had little patience for those who tried to explain away their sins or come to the confessional to justify themselves. These sorts would get a stern rebuke they would not soon forget. But those who came with humility and brokenness, Pio received with sweetness. Whatever approach he took, Padre Pio's favorite moment of any confession was when he pronounced absolution: *"Deínde ego te absólvo a peccátis tuis, in nómine Patris, et Fílii, et Spíritus Sancti. Amen."* It was the moment the power of Christ, working through his poor priesthood, obliterated the sins of men and reconciled them to God.

When Padre Pio finally left the church, a crowd of people followed. They pressed about him, asking for his blessing or for prayers or merely tried to touch him in hopes that somehow God's grace would flow through him. A few friars accompanied Pio, helping to move him through the crowd. Pio smiled, waved, and put his hand on the heads of children thrust in front of him for blessings.

He was profoundly uncomfortable with the attention—and he knew his superiors discouraged such displays. But what could he do? All he did was walk into the street, and a crowd would materialize around him.

No matter what hubbub was going on about him, Pio kept his rosary always wrapped around his hand. His lips constantly moved, mouthing an endless string of Ave Marías and Pater Nosters. Keeping his mind focused on prayer was the only way he could endure the discomforts of such attention.

A reporter from the local newspaper pressed through the crowd, hoping to speak with the famous priest. "Padre Pio!" he shouted, pencil and notebook in hand. "Padre, I have a question for you!"

Pio stopped and turned. "What would you ask of me?"

"Padre," the reporter called, "do you think you are a saint?"

Pio smirked. "My friend, I am just a poor friar who prays."

The winter of 1928 proved to be a very challenging time for Padre Pio. Further decrees from the Holy Office had been issued against him, forbidding him from having any contact with his spiritual director, Padre Benedetto. The Holy See seemed determined to relegate Padre Pio to obscurity. He was still offering Masses in private and still prohibited from engaging in all but the most basic tasks. Painful as this was, Pio handled it all with his characteristic obedience, devoting his time to prayer.

It was a few days before Christmas when Father Serelli came to Pio's cell and informed him he had a visitor.

"But I am not allowed to receive visitors," said Pio.

"Except for family," said Father Serelli, smiling. "You may enter now, Nonna."

Pio's mother appeared in the doorway of the cell.

"Mammella!" Pio said warmly, rising to embrace his mother. "Ah, Mamma Peppa! It is good to see you!"

"I've missed you so much, my boy," she said, her small frame enclosed in her son's strong arms. Pio was now forty-one years old, just entering middle age, with his face becoming wrinkled and the little black that remained in his beard turning to gray. Mamma Peppa was old now, nearly seventy, her face frail and weather-beaten, cracked like old leather from years of peasant life. She nuzzled her old face into Pio's beard and kissed her son affectionately.

"Please enjoy some time with your mother, Pio," Father Serelli said. "She has requested to spend Christmas with us and will be staying in one of the guest rooms for a few days."

"Ah! How lovely!" Pio said, beaming. "It's been so long since I have spent Christmas with my Mammella!"

"It's good to see you smile, Pio," said Father Serelli. "I will see you at vespers."

With that, Pio was left alone with his mother.

Mamma Peppa took her son's gloved hands into her own and ran her wrinkled, bony fingers over his palms. It was a gesture both curious and reverent. "I have heard things about you, my boy," she said weakly.

Pio drew his hands back into the folds of his habit. "I am under obedience to not show my wounds to anybody, save doctors, and only when explicitly commanded."

Mamma Peppa furled her brow. "You think I came here because I wanted to gawk at your hands?"

Pio shuffled uncomfortably. "Well . . . I don't know."

"You are a very holy friar, but sometimes you are still *il gonzo*!" she said, patting his cheek.

"Why have you come, then?" asked Pio.

"Does a mother need an excuse to see her boy? The truth is, I don't know how many winters I have left. I'm old and cold, and your father is dealing with the farm. And . . . well . . . I need to know . . ."

"What do you need to know, Mama?" Pio said, stroking his mother's cheek.

Mamma Peppa dropped to her knees before her son. She clasped his hands in her own and gazed up at him. "Padre, I need to know, how can we be sure that we are not great sinners before God? We do our best, we confess whatever we remember or know, but perhaps it is not enough? Perhaps God sees other things we cannot recall? Perhaps there have been mistakes—"

"—my dear Mammella," Pio said, cutting her off, "if we put into our confession and resolutions all our good will, and we have the intention to confess everything we know or remember, then the mercy of God is so great that he will include and erase even what we cannot remember or know!"

"Are you sure, my boy?" his mother asked tearfully. "Your father and I have done our best, but God is demanding."

"Mama, *you* are demanding, but I never doubted your love for me," said Pio smiling. "There is nothing you and Papa wouldn't have done for me, and God's love for you is so much greater than yours for me. It's about Him," he said, pointing to the crucifix adorning the wall above his bed. "All God wants is sincerity, to do the best with what He has given you. He will take care of the rest. Pray, hope, and don't worry."

Mamma Peppa buried her head in her son's hands and wept. Pio helped her stand and hugged her. "You've done well, Mammella," he said softly. "Heaven will rejoice on the day you enter."

With his mother present, Father Serelli waived the rules to allow Padre Pio to celebrate the Christmas Vigil Mass. It was the first time Padre Pio had said Mass for anyone but the altar servers in a long while. The chapel was cold and clammy, illumined only by the flickering light of the altar candles. Friars glided in silently, taking their places in the choir. Mamma Peppa was seated in the back, in a pew set off to the side typically reserved for visitors. Before the Mass began, she kneeled against the pew before her, hands folded. Some friars noticed she was shaking from the cold and offered her a fur coat.

"Nonsense!" she said. "I don't want to look like a fancy lady, my dears."

"Now we see where Pio gets his stubbornness," the friars snickered.

Mamma Peppa listened to the proclamation of the birth of Jesus Christ by candlelight and received Holy Communion from the hands of her saintly son while the friars chanted hymns in honor of the incarnation of the Son of God. As she knelt in the shadowy pew after Communion, making her act of thanksgiving, it seemed as if heaven were already present. She feasted her eyes at the altar, festooned with festive flowers, glowing warm in the yellow flickering light

Now I can die happy, Lord.

Mamma Peppa's prayer was prophetic. The next day, she fell ill, the chill of the frigid monastery chapel being too much for her. Pio and the friars attended to her bedside constantly, ministering to her bodily and spiritually. Her condition got worse. She was wracked with coughing so severe it seemed like her fragile body would break apart. When her breathing became labored, Dr. Festa was summoned to her bedside. He listened to her wheezing breaths through his stethoscope.

"She has double pneumonia," he pronounced grimly to Pio. "Both lungs are filling up. Prepare for the end. It won't be long."

On January 3, Padre Pio heard his mother's confession and gave her Viaticum, the last Holy Communion a Catholic receives before passing from this world. Mamma Peppa struggled to breathe while Pio held the Eucharist aloft before administering it to her. The friars gathered around the bed prayed silently.

"Food for the journey," she wheezed before receiving the sacred host on her tongue and making the sign of the cross.

"May I be alone with my mother for a moment?" Pio said to his brethren. The friars nodded and filed out of the room. Padre Pio looked at his mother. She was resting now, her eyes closed. Her breathing sounded strange, like a coarse gurgling. The priest removed his hands from the sleeves of his habit. He pulled off the fingerless gloves he wore to hide his stigmata, revealing his mysterious wounds. He pressed his hands—his raw wounds—tenderly to his mother's forehead. He closed his eyes and whispered, "Dear God, thank you for this woman, Maria Giuseppa Di Nunzio Forgione, whom you gave me to be my Mammella. She is coming to you soon. I pray thee receive her in light with all thy saints. Dear Jesus, dear Mary, take care of my Mamma Peppa."

He made the sign of the cross over her, and putting his gloves back on, called the friars back in.

The brothers, led by Pio, sat around her bed, praying the Rosary together. Pio placed a crucifix in her hand. Mamma Peppa drifted in and out, sometimes mouthing Ave Marías with the brothers, sometimes fading off into unconsciousness. While they were praying the Fifth Joyful Mystery of Joseph and Mary being reconciled with Jesus after finding Him in the temple, Mamma Peppa suddenly raised herself up, pressed the crucifix to her lips, kissed it, then dropped back down onto her pillow, unconscious. Her breath stilled; her little body stopped moving up and down.

Padre Pio collapsed at her bedside and began sobbing. "Mammella! Mammella! My beautiful Mammella! My sweet, darling Mammella!" His tears flowed down into his beard. Mammella was no more. Her soul had flown up to God.

CHAPTER 10

Suffering Relieved

Despite the decrees against Padre Pio from Rome, his popularity only increased. Pious Catholics and mere curiosity seekers alike were always milling about the road to Our Lady of Grace in San Giovanni Rotondo, hoping to catch some glimpse of the famous stigmatic. Though Pio's superiors in the monastery supported him, they were vexed by the distractions. All the attention brought Pio a profound sense of embarrassment.

The Capuchin regional superiors decided it was best to move Padre Pio. Orders were sent for his transfer to another friary on the other side of the country. When word spread that he was leaving, the townspeople of San Giovanni Rotondo were furious. They flooded out of their homes, swarmed up the hillside road to Our Lady of Grace, and massed about the front of the monastery. Some waved signs saying, "Keep

Pio in San Giovanni Rotondo!" and "Pio our Saint!" A band of strong young men blockaded the road to the friary, preventing cars from passing by, lest Padre Pio be taken away without their knowledge.

Pio had nothing to do with this commotion. Nonetheless, it reflected poorly on him. The Capuchins wrote to the Holy See, explaining that the situation had become tense and that it was unwise to move Padre Pio. His detractors complained about a "bodyguard" of thugs that always protected Pio. They told the Holy See that they feared violence would break out if Pio were removed.

Faced with such unflattering reports, it was not long before even harsher measures were taken against Padre Pio. A new decree in 1931 stated that he could no longer hear confessions nor have any contact with the faithful whatsoever. Pio's heart broke when he heard of the new decree. He became a priest without a flock, a magnificent confessor forbidden from hearing confessions, a minister of the sacraments with nobody to administer them to. His sole consolation was offering Mass in the friary chapel, with no one present save for a single altar server and of course his Lord in the Eucharist. Pio would gaze lovingly at the crucifix of Christ.

You were alone, cast off, rejected by all. Please help me bear this trial with your patience, O Lord.

Despite his confinement, Pio was not idle. He constantly sought out the best way to serve Christ in whatever circumstance he found himself.

"Lord," he prayed one day in the chapel, "I cannot preach. I cannot baptize. I cannot communicate with the faithful. I cannot even give them the Eucharist. How can I minister to your flock?"

During this difficult time, Padre Pio heard of a laborer from San Giovanni Rotondo who was injured in a mining accident. He had to be sent all the way to Foggia for treatment, but after a week, he was still waiting for medical assistance. There was no room for the poor man in the Foggia hospital, so he had been left in a cot in the hallway, neglected by doctors and in immense suffering.

The tribulation of the poor workman moved Pio's heart with compassion. He knew the hospital in Foggia was too far away and too overcrowded to serve the people of San Giovanni Rotondo. As he prayed about this, Pio's mind was enlightened with an idea. The answer to his prayers came to him like a light from heaven. Ever since he had served as a medic during the war, he had a deep affection for the sick and wounded. Perhaps he could use his abilities to relieve their suffering by building an infirmary in San Giovanni Rotondo.

When he returned to his cell, Pio picked up his Bible and flipped to the twenty-fifth chapter of Matthew's gospel. He read the passage aloud: "I was hungry, and you gave me something to eat. I was thirsty, and you gave me something to drink. I was a stranger, and you invited me in. I needed clothes, and you clothed me. I was sick, and you looked after me. I was in prison, and you came to visit me. Truly, I tell you, whatever you did for one of the least of these brothers and sisters of Mine, you did for Me." The meaning of Christ's words was simple and radical—like Padre Pio himself.

Pio went to see Father Serelli. "Padre, attached to our monastery is an old storage garage that is no longer in use. I would like to convert this into an infirmary for the poor of San Giovanni Rotondo."

Father Serelli raised his eyebrows. "Pio, you know you are not permitted to have contact with the faithful."

"I have no ulterior motive, Padre," Pio said, placing his hand on his heart. "I want only to serve the poor and the sick as Christ commanded."

"People will say it is a publicity stunt."

"It is no such thing!" insisted Pio.

"Even so, people will think it is," replied Father Serelli calmly. "Do you want to draw more attention to yourself and this monastery?"

"Of course not," he said.

"Well, we seem to be at an impasse, then."

Pio paced about the room, deep in prayerful thought. His rosary was wrapped around his gloved hand, his fingers working over the beads while he turned the matter over in his mind. His superior watched him, in awe of the man's depth.

"Padre," Pio said finally, "if I am not permitted to have any contact with the faithful, there is no reason I need to work in the infirmary personally. Other friars can staff the infirmary, or we could ask some of the sisters from the convent in town. I will do the sweeping, the plastering, the repairs, the grimy work. But my name need not be attached to it. This infirmary is not for me—it is for the poor of this village."

Father Serelli said nothing, his hands folded upon his desk.

"If it is not from God, it will fail," Pio added. "What have we to lose? I am a priest; my duty is to minister to those in need. Help me to do so in this small way."

Father Serelli smiled. "Very well, Pio. The storage garage is yours. You may speak to your brethren about helping you and reach out to the sisters at the convent, but I do not want the general public involved. Is that understood?"

"Thank you, Padre," Pio said, bowing. "Yes, of course!"

A rush of excitement began to sweep through the friary as Pio's project took shape. San Giovanni Rotondo was a poor town. Everyone could see that the infirmary was desperately needed.

"This infirmary will be for the poorest of the poor, for those who have no other earthly consolation," Pio told his brethren. "It will be a house for the relief of suffering. We will do our best to minister to the spirit, and medicine will do the rest."

Everyone who heard about the project was eager to help, including laypeople from the town, who contributed money to pay for the expenses.

Pio oversaw the transformation of the building into the infirmary. In his free time, he could be found on a stepladder, dirty smock over his monastic habit, a bucket in hand, slathering fresh plaster upon the walls. He organized the work crews to carry in and assemble the dozen beds the infirmary would hold. And he was very particular about the color of paint used in the room.

"No! Not white!" he said, annoyed when a young novice suggested it.

"Why not white?" said the novice. "All hospitals are white."

"That's exactly the problem! White is so cold, so sanitary. White walls. White sheets. White doctor's coats. I don't want our patients to feel like they are in a laboratory."

"Well, what color paint should I get?" asked the novice.

"Something soft. Delicate. Pastels. Light green? Yellow? Think . . . soothing."

As the novice nodded and scurried off to carry out Pio's wishes, an electrician wiring the room for light called from a ladder overhead, "Hey Padre, what kind of lights you want in here? Standard hospital lights?"

"No," said Pio, "those are too . . . clinical. Something softer. We need it well-lit in here, but soft light."

Before the year's end, the infirmary was open, serving the most destitute. Several local doctors came forward to volunteer their services, taking turns staffing the clinic. No pay was accepted or expected; care was offered for free to any who needed it. The infirmary became a blessing to the community. Before long, there was chatter about expanding it to turn it into a proper hospital.

"I told you that you had nothing to worry about," Pio playfully taunted Father Serelli.

Indeed, things were finally beginning to look up for Padre Pio. In 1933, he was notified that the Holy Office had reversed its decisions about him. He was again allowed to say public Masses, preach, hear confessions, and exercise a normal priestly ministry. Letters had flooded Rome with testimonies of the good works of Padre Pio, the success of the infirmary, and other witnesses to the friar's holiness. Eventually, Pope Pius XI said, "I have never been badly disposed toward Padre Pio, though it seems I have been badly informed."

Just like that, after over a decade of restrictions, Padre Pio was free!

As Padre Pio resumed his ministry, visitors were again permitted limited access to the monastery. Quite a few of these visitors were other clergy who had heard of the stigmatist of San Giovanni Rotondo and were eager to satisfy their curiosity. Once, an eminent Italian bishop came to the friary to meet Padre Pio. This particular bishop was a thoroughly modern man, enamored with the latest theories and giving little weight to tales of supernatural marvels.

While he ate dinner with the friars, he was served by Padre Pio. The bishop was impressed with Pio's humility. Scurrying about the dining hall with a smock on, Pio waited on his brethren in silence as if he were a servant.

He does not seem arrogant, thought the bishop. *He seems to be a model friar. He carries dishes and cleans up like any novice.*

Despite this, he couldn't help but notice that Pio's face was marred by a swollen purple cheek and crusts of blood on his lip and nose. It looked as though he had been assaulted!

"Padre Pio," said the bishop, "you seem to be wounded. Did you injure yourself while working on your infirmary?"

Pio stopped and touched his face. "I apologize, your Excellency. I was not aware my wounds were so visible." Turning to Father Serelli, Pio said, "Padre, may I be excused to clean up?"

Father Serelli nodded. Pio took off his smock and disappeared down the corridor. An awkward silence filled the dining hall in his absence. The bishop shuffled about in his seat, perplexed.

"Well, Father Serelli," the bishop finally said, "Pio was certainly diplomatic in avoiding my question."

Father Serelli smiled and said nothing, taking a bite of his cabbage soup. Then dabbing his mouth with a handkerchief, said, "I don't know if you would believe me if I told you, Your Excellency."

The other friars smirked, keeping their eyes cast down.

"Will someone tell me what is going on here?" the bishop said, looking about.

"Fra Roberto," Father Serelli gestured to one of the friars, "you sleep adjacent to Pio's cell. Please tell the good bishop how Padre Pio received those wounds."

"Yes, Padre," said Fra Roberto meekly. "You see, Your Excellency, Padre Pio gets, well . . ." the friar stammered.

"He gets what?" inquired the bishop.

Everyone was staring at Fra Roberto. The young brother shifted about uncomfortably. "He gets beaten up by the devil," he finally blurted out.

The bishop erupted into laughter. But his jovial tone faded when he saw no one else found this amusing. He collected himself. "Surely, you cannot be serious?" the bishop demanded. "The devil physically beating up a friar such that he comes to meals with his face bloodied?"

"That's all I know, Your Excellency," Fra Roberto said, looking down into his soup.

The bishop turned to Father Serelli. "Is this something you condone?"

"When you are dealing with Padre Pio, you must expect the unexpected," answered Father Serelli.

The bishop sat back in his chair with a haughty grin. "You do love your fabulous medieval tales up here, don't you?"

"If you say so, Your Excellency," replied Father Serelli, provoking laughter from the other friars.

The dinner continued in a more subdued tone, until suddenly, the ceiling began to vibrate with a low rumbling sound. The friars all paused. The bishop turned pale. Banging and clanking came from behind the walls. The friars all made the sign of the cross.

The bishop looked about incredulously. "Now, Pio is playing tricks on me! You expect me to believe these noises are the devil? It's just Padre Pio having a bit of—"

At that moment, Pio walked through the door, his face cleaned of the blood. Unaware of the discussion or the commotion, Pio donned his smock and began waiting the table. A moment later, the ceiling rumbled again.

The bishop felt a cold chill grip him. The man threw up his hands. "You've convinced me!" he said, trembling. He stood up quickly, and bowing, said, "Thank you for your hospitality, Padre Serelli. I will see myself out."

And so, things went well for Padre Pio for several years. Letters again poured into the monastery, his Masses were packed, and his confession lines stretched out the door of the church. Occasional visitors came to seek his advice or to merely gaze at the mysterious friar. And yes, occasionally the devil beat him up.

The hospital grew as well, with people coming from all over the region for medical care. There was talk of expanding the clinic, building a larger structure on the hillside of San Giovanni Rotondo that would be a proper hospital.

But unfortunately, the changing events unfolding in Italy would postpone Pio's plans for expanding the clinic. It was September 3, 1939, a Sunday. Padre Pio had just finished celebrating Mass in the parish church in town. He noticed a commotion outside in the street. After making his customary thanksgiving, he went out to see what was going on.

"Padre! Padre!" people cried out, running up to him in agitation. "What is going to happen?"

"What is this all about?" Pio said.

"Look, Padre!" a man said, thrusting a newspaper into the priest's hands. Pio squinted and read the headline. *GERMANY INVADES POLAND*. Pio's heart sank. He remembered the horrors of the Great War twenty years earlier, how it had destroyed so many lives and uprooted so many people.

"Let us pray we stay out of it," he said, handing the paper back to the man.

"But Italy has made an alliance with Germany!" someone shouted. "If this war spreads, Hitler's war will become our war!"

"Padre, what should we do?" a woman cried. There was a frenzy of concern as people jostled to look at the paper. Pio could see looks of panic on their faces. In his right hand as always, he fingered his rosary beads, silently imploring the Blessed Mother for help as he pondered what to say.

"Will they bomb San Giovanni Rotondo?" someone asked.

"Not a single bomb will fall on San Giovanni Rotondo," Pio said, raising his voice over the din. The crowd fell quiet at the booming sound of the priest's voice. "Listen to me," he said, holding aloft his gloved hand, "this is in God's hands. The best we can do now is pray for peace and that, if possible, Italy stays out of this conflict. But if we do go to war, I promise you, we will be all right. No harm will befall this city."

Nobody asked Padre Pio how he knew this. The people of San Giovanni Rotondo had learned to not question Pio when he told them how things would be.

CHAPTER 11

Peace Amidst Suffering

American General Nathan Twining was speechless. Before him stood two US Airforce captains, sheepishly holding their caps in their hands like children. The general paced back and forth before his desk, rubbing his head. Strewn with papers and schematics, his desktop contained maps of Allied bombing targets in southern Italy. One map featured San Giovanni Rotondo with a red circle drawn around it.

"Let me get this straight," he said gruffly, "because this is going in the official report, and I want to make sure I'm understanding this correctly." The two captains nodded and shifted uncomfortably. "Last week, we received intel that the Germans may be maintaining a weapons cache at San Giovanni Rotondo. You two were to command a bombing run from Puglia to San Giovanni Rotondo to destroy the town. But when you got to your target . . . and here's where things get a little hazy for me . . ." The general cleared his throat. "You, eh, you say you saw a flying monk?"

"That's correct, General Twining," said one of the captains. "As we approached the target, we saw . . . a vision . . . an apparition . . . I don't know what to call it. But it was some kind of monk flying in front of our aircrafts."

"You saw this, too, Captain Delaney?" asked the General.

"Yes, sir, I did. It's as Captain Hufford said. We both saw it. So did our men."

"And this monk, he was not in any sort of aircraft?"

"No, sir," said the captains in unison.

"All right," General Twining said, "so the monk appeared in the air, and you say he held his hands up as if telling you to stop?"

"That's correct, sir."

"What happened next?"

"Well," Captain Hufford continued, "I thought I was seeing things, so I didn't pay it much heed at first. Of course, I didn't realize Captain Delaney and the others were seeing the same thing. Anyhow, we continued on our way, and when we approached the target . . ."

"Go on," urged the general.

"We had an equipment malfunction," Captain Delaney interjected. "Our bombing doors wouldn't open."

"Whose bombing doors? Yours?"

The two captains looked at each other, then at the general. "None of them," they said.

"So, every one of the fighters in your squadron had a 'malfunction'? Every bombing door refused to open . . . *simultaneously*?"

"That's correct, sir," said Hufford.

General Twining pounded his desk. "That is the most ridiculous story I've ever heard! And believe me, I've heard some whoppers. Seems to me like you boys fouled up big and you're hiding something from me. Don't think I won't get to the bottom of this! I'm not going to let you embarrass the Fifteenth Airforce and make me look like a fool!"

The general took a breath and composed himself. His face was red, and the veins in his neck were bulging.

"But," he continued, more measured now, "for now, orders are orders. We've got a war to win. You're going back to San Giovanni Rotondo on another run, and this time I'm coming with you!"

The following day, the American squadron was back in the sky again, enroute to San Giovanni Rotondo. General Twining was in command, leading five B-17 "Flying Fortress" bombers toward the little mountainside town where American intelligence insisted the Nazis were secretly storing weapons.

"Approaching target area," Twining said into his headset.

"Roger that," crackled the voices of the other pilots over the radio.

"We're heading into San Giovanni Rotondo north by northeast," said the general's assistant. "Target will be in sight in five minutes."

"Thank you, Lieutenant," said Twining. He looked out over the fields that fanned out around San Giovanni Rotondo. "Peaceful place," he mused. "Too bad the Germans got these people all mixed up in this. When we're done, this place is going to be in so many pieces that God himself won't be able to find it on judgment day."

"Sir, we're approaching the target," said the lieutenant. Twining could see the small town; from the air, it looked pathetic, a negligible assortment of stone houses clustered on a lonely hillside.

"All right, gentlemen, we're gonna do this smooth and in a single pass. Sweep in low from the south side, wait for my word to drop—"

The general stopped, his jaw hanging open. It couldn't be. In the clear blue sky before his bomber, the image of a monk floated in the air, arms held aloft.

The radio erupted with chatter from the other pilots. "Do you see him, General?"

The lieutenant made the sign of the cross.

"I don't believe it," General Twining said to himself more than to anyone else.

Immediately, there was a loud clank, the sound of the bombing doors opening.

"Lieutenant, why are we dropping our payload?" shouted the general. "We're not over target!"

"I . . . I don't know! I didn't release the hatch!" The bombs of General Twining's B-17 fell from the open bomber doors over the fields outside San Giovanni Rotondo, thudding harmlessly into the soil. They didn't even explode.

"Who gave the order to drop? Why are we dropping?" cried out the other pilots over the radio. From the window, Twining could see that all the other bombers were dropping their bombs over the fields as well.

"Abort mission! Abort mission!" Twining cried into the headset. The planes turned and headed back to the airfields in Bari as the people of San Giovanni Rotondo continued on with their sleepy lives.

Thus was the town of San Giovanni Rotondo spared from the horrors of World War II, just as Pio had predicted. Stories of the "Flying Monk" circulated around the US Airforce, such that some of the Protestant airmen who witnessed the prodigy converted to Catholicism because of it.

As the war was winding down in summer of 1945, General Twining heard about the stigmatic friar of San Giovanni Rotondo. The general decided to pay a visit to the monastery to meet this mysterious monk. As Twining walked up the gravel pathway to the monastery, he saw a group of friars coming to meet him. He gasped! At the head of the delegation was the same monk he had seen in the sky—a stocky friar with powerful, dark eyebrows, a dark mustache, a gray bread, and a tuft of silver hair atop his head. Twining froze as if in a daze.

Padre Pio walked up to Twining with a jovial smile. He extended his gloved hand in greeting. "So, you're the one who wanted to destroy everything?"

Twining hesitated. "I . . . I . . ." He grabbed Pio's gloved hand with his, without even realizing it, shaking it slowly.

"It's a good thing you didn't," said Pio, "there never was any German ammo facility here. It was only a rumor."

A tear crept out of General Twining's eye. What could he say in return? And yet Padre Pio held no contempt for the soldier, and the two became lifelong friends.

By the war's end in August of 1945, Pio was fifty-eight years old and had built up a reputation that went beyond Italy. People from all over the world were eager to write and visit the friar of San Giovanni Rotondo. His confession lines stretched into the hundreds, but Pio never denied penitents access to the reconciliation of God. Sometimes, he spent up to ten hours in the confessional, listening to men and women pour out their sins before God, pleading for his mercy. So many people came to him for confession that a rule was instituted, prohibiting a person from returning to him for confession again unless he or she had waited eight days. Eventually, people were required to make appointments over a month in advance.

Pio was a generous confessor but also took no nonsense. He had a gift for reading the hearts of his penitents. If a man confessed insincerely, Pio was known to chastise him and tell him to return when he was truly sorry. It was impossible to deceive him. Once, a scrupulous man wanted to confess to Padre Pio even though it had been less than eight days since his last confession. When he knelt in the confessional, Pio said, "How long has it been since your last confession?"

"Three weeks," the man said, lying to the priest.

There was silence from the other side of the grille.

"Why do you waste my time and offend God with your lies? Get out of here! Bear fruits worthy of repentance."

Stunned, the man stumbled out of the confessional. A few moments later, he was found wandering about the walls outside the friary, sobbing. A few brothers found the man and asked him what was wrong.

"I've told many lies during my lifetime!" he cried. "I thought I could deceive Padre Pio, too."

The man later made a sincere confession and went to Mass and Holy Communion every day for the rest of his life.

Another time, a woman entered the confessional dressed immodestly, with more skin showing than covered. She began with the sign of the cross, but before she got a chance to say anything, Pio's gruff voice came from behind the grille. "Go away."

"Excuse me?" asked the woman.

"Go away and get dressed! How careless!"

The woman stormed out in a huff, complaining about the friar's rudeness. After confessions, another Capuchin friar approached Padre Pio and said, "Was it wise to discourage her, Padre? Sometimes, souls are better treated with sweetness."

Pio shrugged. "I do not give sweets to someone who needs a laxative. A soul in need of being shaken up should not be caressed."

As Pio provided medicine to the soul, his infirmary provided care for the body. It grew considerably over time, such that by the outbreak of the war, it had become clear it would have to be expanded into a proper hospital. Local people contributed to the project, and doctors volunteered their time. Padre Pio selected a site for the expansion, a rocky eminence jutting off the side of Mount Gargano. But there were simply not enough funds to begin construction. After all, San Giovanni Rotondo was a poor town, and all of Italy was impoverished after the chaos of World War II. Padre Pio prayed and pondered this as he walked amongst the stones where he imagined his new hospital.

God will make a way.

Not long after, a group of doctors from Foggia came to visit Padre Pio at the monastery and talk to him about his work. Pio explained that the hospital would be called *Casa Sollievo della Sofferenza*, that is, *Home for Relief of Suffering.* One of the men, a Dr. Guglielmo Sanguinetti, expressed amazement. "Padre, we support your vision, but . . . let's be realistic. Build a hospital now? When Italy is in shambles and the economy shattered? Where will you get the money? You can't squeeze water from stones."

Padre Pio stared into Dr. Sanguinetti's eyes with a deep, piercing look. "You will come live at San Giovanni Rotondo," he said. "You will be of much help."

Dr. Sanguinetti laughed awkwardly but could not contain his incredulity. "How can I help? I'm poor just like everybody else. Besides, I can't move here. I can't afford to retire from my work. I can't collect my pension yet."

Padre Pio looked upward as if appealing to heaven. "Well, there is the ticket, don't forget that." Then pressing his finger into the doctor's chest, he said, "And you will live here, I am telling you that!"

Dr. Sanguinetti lost his composure. "Ticket! What ticket!? What are you talking about?"

Padre Pio inexplicably ignored the question and moved on to discuss other matters. Dr. Sanguinetti returned home to his work in a daze, pondering Padre Pio's request and his strange comments. He was bothered at the friar's presumption, assuming that he would pick up his life and move to San Giovanni Rotondo.

Then, one day, Dr. Sanguinette had a revelation, realizing what "ticket" Padre Pio was referring to. After World War II, the Italian government sold bonds to its people to raise money for reconstruction. These bonds were like lottery tickets, which were entered into a drawing. Anyone whose bond number was drawn would win a prize. Dr. Sanguinetti was notified that his bond ticket had been chosen, and he had won a small fortune. It was enough money for him to retire and move to San Giovanni Rotondo, just as Pio had said.

But the marvels would not stop there. As Dr. Sanguinetti was closing up his office and preparing to move, he paid a visit to a wealthy patient, a nobleman named Marquis Sacchetti. When the doctor told Sacchetti everything that happened, Marquis donated a vast amount of his fortune to the *Casa Sollievo della Sofferenza* project and even collected donations from his wealthy friends. Padre Pio now had the people and resources he needed to get his hospital.

The project officially began on October 5, 1946, when papers were filed with the Italian government to establish the hospital. The statutes of *Casa Sollievo della Sofferenza* declared that the mission of the hospital was "to receive any person who appeals for assistance and charity in the name of Christ." The incorporation of the hospital was a huge step; it gave the project an "official" status, no longer just the wild dream of a mystic friar. Donations began pouring in from everywhere. American soldiers stationed in Italy were eager to help, as they had been inspired by Pio's saintliness—and perhaps heard the tales of the flying monk. A network of Pio's supporters within the United States were able to raise considerable sums as well. The Italian government, too, donated 250 million lire to *Casa Sollievo della Sofferenza.*

Even as the hospital grew and it seemed many were finding care through Pio's work, there was one soul who seemed to be nearing the end of his journey.

After the death of Mamma Peppa, Padre Pio's father, Grazio, had moved to San Giovanni Rotondo to be closer to his famous son, lodging in a hostel for the old and poor. Grazio, now eighty-five, was a wizened old man with face cracked from years of squinting in the sun and a shock of white hair atop his head. He, too, was something of a celebrity in town. As he shuffled to and from Mass or the market, people would greet him and compliment him on his holy son. The old farmer would shrug and say, "I didn't make him what he is. Jesus Christ did."

One October day, some townspeople came to fetch Padre Pio from the monastery to bring him to his dying father. Pio came to Grazio's side at once, his rosary wrapped around his gloved hand, praying the entire way. He found his father resting quietly on a simple cot. The old man's breathing was thin and wheezing, his forehead beaded with sweat.

"Hello, Papa," Pio said, kneeling beside the cot.

Grazio turned and squinted. "Ah, Francesco . . ." he said weakly.

"It's been a long time since anyone has called me that," Pio said, taking his father by the hand and kissing it.

"God has been good to us. Good to our family."

"You've done well, Papa. God will be happy to see you."

"What if I'm not ready?" Grazio's voice trembled. He was speaking now not as a father to his son but as a dying man to a priest. "I've committed many sins in my life, Francesco. How do I know God will forgive me?"

"That's what I am here for now, Papa," answered Pio, smiling sweetly. And with that, he made the sign of the cross over Grazio and heard his father's last confession. Then, as he had done years ago with his mother, he gave Grazio Holy Viaticum. "Be at peace, Papa," Pio said to the old man.

Grazio seemed to find comfort. His shoulders relaxed. He breathed easier.

"Son," said Grazio, "life is hard, full of troubles, full of suffering."

Pio nodded, wiping a tear from his eye.

"But it's also beautiful," the old man replied.

"Are you asking me or telling me?" said Pio.

"Both," Grazio smiled.

"You speak truth, Papa. You suffered for Mammella and for me, for our whole family. You decreased yourself so that we might increase. Your life has been hard. But beautiful. Everything that comes from God's hand is beautiful."

"And *good*," Grazio stressed. Then sighing wistfully, he said, "It seemed to all go by so fast. But I am ready to go."

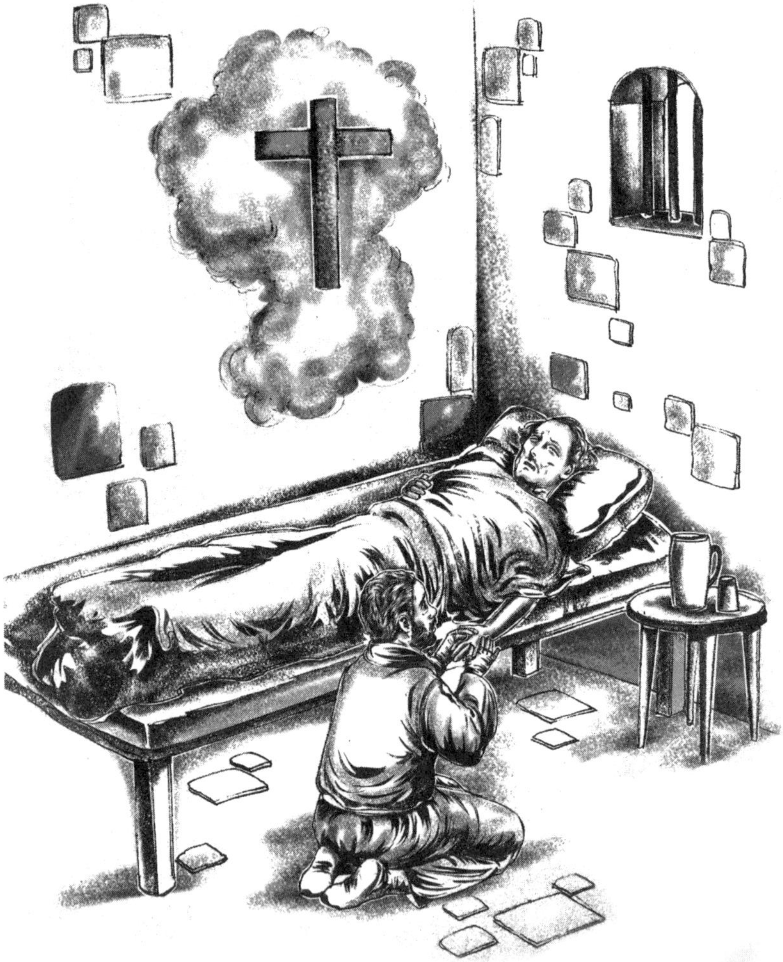

"Man is like a breath, and his days are like a passing shadow," Pio quoted the Psalms. Even as he talked with Grazio, Pio kept his rosary wrapped tightly in his hand, silently praying Ave Marías in an endless litany for his father's soul.

Grazio was clutching a crucifix that Pio had placed on the old man's chest. His eyes were closed now, his cracked lips moving noiselessly as he mouthed prayers in the presence of his son. Pio stared at his father's withered hands, the skin so wrinkly it looked like it clung to the man's bone like old rags.

He truly worked his fingers raw for us.

"I'm proud of you, my boy, *il mio ragazzo*," the old man whispered without opening his eyes. And with that, Grazio let out a deep, long breath and fell still.

When Pio realized he was gone, he leaned in and kissed Grazio's crinkled forehead, already stiff and clammy. Pio sat back and thought about his memories of his father, of the pride on Grazio's face whenever he would attend one of Pio's Masses, the way his father traveled around the world *twice* to provide for Pio's novitiate. He recalled the sight of his father, pack slung over his shoulder, walking away down the birch-lined path to Benevento that bright spring day so long ago when Grazio first left for America. Pio smiled and wiped tears from his eyes.

Then his mind drifted back even earlier to more tender memories: sitting on Grazio's lap as a boy, enfolded in his father's arms and reposing in the orange glow of the fire as his family prayed the Rosary; walking with him and listening to him banter excitedly with the other villagers about things Pio didn't understand—he just liked hearing his father's voice; strolling the flagstone path from Pietrelcina to the farm in the pink light of the early morning. Pio remembered being a toddler, sitting atop Grazio's shoulders when his father was young and strong. Grazio would work the plow in the fields of Piana Romana, with his tiny son straddled atop his broad shoulders, laughing and rejoicing in the brightness of the sun, the freshness of the air, the greenness of creation, happy and innocent as the day Adam first opened his eyes and blinked in the light of paradise.

At the thought of it, Pio convulsed and sunk down onto the floor beside the bed, sobbing. "Papa!" he cried. "My Papa!" The floodgates of his heart opened. Tears flowed down his gray-streaked beard.

Several minutes later, Pio composed himself and left the room, searching for the town coroner to notify him of Grazio's death. People came and went. There were condolences and hushed conversations about the funeral Mass. When all these details were settled, Pio slipped into the parish church to pray. He lit a candle before the altar of Saint Joseph, then making the sign of the cross, he lifted his eyes to heaven and said, "I've no father now but you, Lord."

CHAPTER 12

Every Man Alone with God

PIO SAT HUNCHED over, staring at his hands. He marveled at the wrinkles and creases that graced them. "Ah, Lord, has it already been so long?" he said.

In most respects, they looked like the hands of any older man, save for the bright red wounds that stared back from his palms like two eyes. Pio had never quite gotten used to seeing them. It was such an odd feeling—to be in the presence of an impenetrable mystery, to marvel at something wondrous, beyond the bounds of human science or reason to explain, and yet the marvel is part of your own body. Pio was as baffled by it as any of his admirers, and no one wondered at it more than he. He gently touched his finger to one of the wounds. It was raw and painful; he drew back.

"Padre, everyone is waiting for you!" someone called from outside the hall.

"I'll be there in a moment," Pio responded, hastily returning his gloves to his hands, again shrouding the mystery from human sight. He knelt on the freshly laid tile floor and made the sign of the cross.

"Sweet Christ, this hospital is your work from beginning to end. The idea was born of the contemplation of your suffering in the poor, and it was through your goodness that the resources were made available. I offer this all to you, most lovable Lord. Help your servant, I pray, to be a worthy steward of these things, weak and sinful though I am. Amen."

The priest stood up with a groan, his knees aching. But then looking up at the crucifix hanging in the hospital corridor, he thought with a smile, *Eh, I have nothing to complain about.*

A moment later, he emerged from one of the side doors of the new *Casa Sollievo della Sofferenza* hospital and shuffled around to the front of the facility. A vast throng of people crowded the front steps of the building where an altar had been assembled the night before. Today, May 5, 1956, the hospital was to be officially opened with a Mass offered by Padre Pio.

The crowds erupted in applause at the sight of him. The priest waved but kept his head downcast. Pio never craved the attention people gave him; it made him feel awkward and unworthy. He diverted attention from himself by greeting Cardinal Lercaro and the entourage of bishops, priests, religious, and government officials who had come to the ceremony. Pio smiled and shook hands with so many people he could not keep track of them. But never once did he stop the train of prayer running through his mind: *Ave María, grátia plena, Dóminus tecum. Benedicta tu in muliéribus . . .*

Even in the midst of so many people—the local papers later estimated 15,000 in attendance—Padre Pio felt God's presence keenly. As he offered Mass and held the Eucharist aloft, gazing in wonder as the bread become his Lord, everything seemed to vanish except for himself and Christ. Alone with Jesus. The phrase struck Pio.

Every person is truly alone with God their entire lives. God is always present to our thoughts, our feelings, our innermost desires. We are always alone with God. Seeking God in the solitude of the cell or a mountain or the chapel . . . these moments don't make us alone with God. They merely remind us that we are alone with Him. Always alone with Him.

After the Mass, Pio spoke briefly. "I thank the benefactors of the whole world who have contributed to the construction of the House for Relief of Suffering. May it become a center of the Franciscan spirit in action, a place of prayer and science where the human race finds itself in Christ crucified as a single flock under one Shepherd. May Our Blessed Lady of All Graces and our Seraphic Father, Saint Francis in heaven, and the Vicar of Christ on earth intercede for us that these wishes may be accomplished."

More applause erupted as Pio quickly ducked behind the podium back to his seat. Cardinal Lercaro spoke next, giving the papal blessing of Pius XII. Then the Mayor of San Giovanni Rotondo spoke, then the head of the local medical association, and on and on. Pio gazed out past the crowds, past the rows of stone houses with their white, crumbling plaster façades, out upon the windswept fields below Gargano's brooding slopes—and beyond them, to the distant purple hills and the eternal blue sky, where beyond it waited the vault of heaven.

Every man alone with God.

"Pio?"

Padre Pio blinked. The mayor was standing before him, holding out a pair of scissors. "It's time to cut the ribbon, Padre."

Photographers and reporters crowded around, gawking at Pio and blinding him with the assault of flashing camera bulbs. Despite feeling overwhelmed, Pio did his best to smile as he made his way to the front doors of the facility. He cut the ribbon to the thunderous cheers of the crowd.

Together with Cardinal Lercaro, Pio and the delegation walked throughout the wings of the hospital, blessing the various rooms and departments. Beside Pio was Dr. Guglielmo Sanguinetti, who years earlier had scoffed at the idea of moving to San Giovanni Rotondo to work for the hospital. Now his face was beaming with pride. "Padre," he said, clutching Pio's arm like an excited boy at a carnival, "this is magnificent! This is beyond my wildest expectation. The hospital in Foggia isn't even this nice!"

"I planted, others watered, and God gave the increase," Padre Pio said.

"Don't be so modest, Pio! This is amazing! Two wings, five stories. A department dedicated to the study and treatment of heart disease. The personal doctor of President Dwight Eisenhower is here! You should be proud of yourself!"

Pio looked at the doctor. "This can only succeed if we learn to be forgetful of self. We must bow down to the sufferings and wounds of our fellow men—make them our own, knowing how to suffer with them for the love of God."

"Well, yes, but—"

"—instill hope in their hearts and bring back a smile to their lips! Restore the ray of light to their souls. Then we shall be offering God the most beautiful, the most noble of prayers, because our prayer will have sprung from sacrifice!"

The doctor smiled. "Of course, Padre. Of course."

Padre Pio was a humble man and understandably reluctant to take any credit for these accomplishments. He merely wanted people to love and honor God. The rest was all secondary to him. But people knew that Padre Pio was something special. They sought him out because of the profound simplicity and intensity of his love for God. They were always swarming about him, surging into his Masses, waiting months to confess to him, crowding about him in the street when he went out, and flooding his monastery with letters.

Though he wanted nothing to do with fame, Padre Pio was now a worldwide celebrity. The Capuchins had to take drastic measures to secure his privacy and to prevent the throngs of adoring faithful from infringing upon his life and the duties he had to fulfill. An iron rail and barrier were installed around his confessional to check the ceaseless flow of penitents. Friars were assigned to accompany Padre Pio at all times to help him navigate the crowds. The number of letters that flooded into Our Lady of Grace monastery was so monumental that his superiors forbid him from answering except in the most cursory manner possible. When Pio did respond, he usually just encouraged people to pray. Catholics were inspired by Pio's encouragement. All over the world, "Padre Pio Prayer Groups" were formed to emulate his spirit and way of life.

In the past, Pio had been persecuted for his stigmata. Now, a new wave of persecution arose against him, driven by the media and the enemies of the Church, who viewed Pio as a conman, an opportunist who was just looking for attention and money. Even the success of his hospital became an occasion for criticism. An Italian newspaper published an article attacking Padre Pio. "Greedy Monk Milks Ignorant Faithful Out of Millions!" the sensational headline read. Other articles in newspapers and magazines followed, accusing Padre Pio of stealing the donations of *Casa Sollievo della Sofferenza.*

The accusations were entirely false, but they nonetheless grieved Pio's heart. He came trudging into the friary chapel, carrying the newspapers and magazines in his gloved fist. Laying them before the altar, Pio dropped to his knees, touched his head to the floor. and prayed the twenty-sixth Psalm: "Vindicate me, O Lord, for I have walked in my integrity, and I have trusted in the Lord without wavering. Prove me, O Lord, and try me; test my heart and my mind. For thy steadfast love is before my eyes, and I walk in faithfulness to thee."

Tears welled in his eyes and drained down his cheeks through the gray hairs of his beard. He wept not so much for his own reputation but that the work of the hospital was being called into question. "Let them destroy me, O Lord, but spare the hospital!"

At first, the Church stood up for Pio. Pope Pius XII had even given Padre Pio a dispensation from his vow of poverty. This allowed him to manage the vast amounts of money that poured in for the hospital. But the persecution did not stop—from 1959 on, the attacks against Padre Pio in the press became relentless. They began accusing him of breaking his vows of chastity, engaging in shameful conduct with the women who confessed to him. The new pope, John XXIII, misinformed about Pio's character, did not think well of the friar. A foreboding shadow seemed to hover over San Giovanni Rotondo as the ecclesiastical authorities distanced themselves from the famous friar.

Finally, the heavy hand of the Church dropped against Padre Pio again. Throughout 1960, Pio was visited nine times by Father Carlo Maccari, Secretary-General of the Diocese of Rome. He interrogated Pio relentlessly, trying to prove that the friar had broken his Capuchin vows by engaging in lewd acts with women. Pio sat calmly, answering Father Maccari's questions in brief, terse answers. Pio could tell that Maccari wished him ill and did not go out of his way to give his inquisitor any information he didn't have to. He behaved with the characteristic Forgione stubbornness bequeathed to him by his mother.

The interrogations were a slow crucifixion for Pio. He was no stranger to being probed and questioned and was able to submit in obedience. But it still caused him immense suffering. Now an old man, Pio thought such days were far behind him. His old friend and one-time confessor Padre Agostino came to visit him in his cell to console Pio.

"They hate what you represent, Pio. Things are not as they used to be. There are many men in the Church who are enamored with everything new. Science. Progress. Psychology. New theology. New . . . *everything*. But you? You are not new. You are medieval. A friar who sleeps on a board, carries the wounds of Christ, and encourages people to pray? You don't fit into their new vision."

"What will be will be," said Pio, shrugging.

"Pio, don't be so dense! They are crushing you!"

"Sweet is the hand of the Church, even when she strikes," Pio responded with a smile, "for it is the hand of one's mother."

"You aren't going to protest this at all?" demanded Agostino.

Pio furled his whitened brows, thinking deeply. "Well, they told me I have to keep my Masses under a half hour."

Agostino laughed. "Your prayer of consecration alone takes a half hour."

"God knows how much I would like to be able to say Mass freely like any other priest. But I can't do it," he said with resignation.

"They are trying to destroy you, Pio."

Pio looked up at the crucifix which had adorned the wall of his cell for decades. It was old and scuffed. The face of Christ was not stoic or asleep like in so many depictions; rather, the mouth was agape in pain, eyes half opened, existing in the liminal realm between life and death. The body of

Christ hung low, seeming to sag beneath the weight of the world's sins. Pio was silent for a moment.

"I think they are trying to put a gravestone over San Giovanni Rotondo," he finally said. "But they have not been successful because the finger of God is here."

By autumn of 1960, the apostolic visitation of Father Maccari was complete, and his report was submitted to Rome. The document read by Pope John XXIII was scathing in its condemnation of Padre Pio.

"The character of Padre Pio is devious," he wrote. "Reticence. Narrowness of mind. Outright lies. These are the weapons Pio uses to evade my questions! My overall impression of the man? Pathetic. The religious atmosphere of San Giovanni Rotondo is somewhere between superstition and magic. The powers and importance the people attribute to this man are beyond belief. His supporters are a vast, dangerous organization. I don't understand how such an elaborate deception could be permitted to grow in San Giovanni Rotondo so long unchecked."

Pope John read Maccari's report with great interest and deduced that Padre Pio was a sham. Armed with Maccari's testimony, the Church began preparing a sweeping new crackdown on Padre Pio.

Perhaps Padre Agostino was right that Pio was a bit naïve about the situation. Pio soon got a shocking demonstration of how eagerly his enemies wanted to destroy him. One day, he was sitting in his confessional. He had just finished absolving a penitent and had his head bowed in prayer when he noticed a tiny black ball nestled into the corner of his confessional. It was hard to make it out in the shadows. Pio knelt and picked it up. It was soft in his hands like foam. When he tugged on it, he found it was attached to a wire that led behind the baseboard around the floor of his confessional. It took him a moment to realize it was a little microphone attached to a cord.

Pio got on his knees and pried the baseboard molding from the wall, revealing even more wire that led to a second microphone tucked in the corner behind his seat. He yanked the cord off and stormed off to Father Romano's office.

"Someone has wiretapped my confessional!" he cried, dropping the ball of wire and microphones upon the desk of his superior. "Who would do such a wicked thing?"

Father Romano, a middle-aged friar with spectacles and a pointed black beard, looked at the wires skeptically. "Padre, I understand you are frustrated, but—"

"—I pulled them out of there myself! Surely, no cleric would do this? The seal of the confessional is sacred! This is a grave sin!"

"Pio," said Father Romano sternly, "we have some bigger issues to discuss."

"What is of greater import than someone wiretapping the confessional of one of your priests?"

"This came from Rome today," said Father Romano, handing a letter to Pio. Pio squinted at the tiny print, dug around in his pocket, and put on a pair of reading glasses. He mouthed the words as he read, "In light of the report of Father Carlo Maccari on the life and ministry of Padre Pio of San Giovanni Rotondo, the Holy Office, with the support of

His Holiness Pope John XXIII and in conjunction with the provincial superiors of the Capuchin province of Foggia, decrees the following restrictions be enacted against Padre Pio:

1. No one is to be allowed to confess to Padre Pio more than once per month.
2. Padre Pio is to be removed from the board of *Casa Sollievo della Sofferenza*. He is to have no direct involvement with the hospital.
3. The superior of Our Lady of Grace, Father Romano, is to be removed and a new superior chosen from outside the region.
4. The Capuchin brothers of Our Lady of Grace who have spent years in the company of Padre Pio are to be relocated to other friaries outside the region.

Pio looked up, speechless.

"They have given up trying to destroy you, Pio," said Father Romano blandly. "Now, they are going to simply dismantle our monastery. I am to be relocated, along with all of our longest-serving brothers."

Pio's body shook. He fell to his knees and dropped his head, thumping it roughly against the superior's desk. "I'm sorry, Father! I have brought all this trouble upon you! You do not deserve this!"

Pio was used to suffering. His whole life had been one trial after another, a long series of attacks, misunderstandings, prejudices. Just as he had accepted the mysterious wounds imprinted upon his body so many years ago, so had he passively acquiesced to all the hardship inflicted upon him. But

an attack upon his brethren, upon his superior, upon faithful men who had nothing to do with his own matters, that was a new kind of pain.

"I'm sorry, Father! Tell me what you would have me do," he begged.

"I think you need to have a meeting with the board of the hospital," his superior said coldly. "Tell them you are resigning. I will phone them to arrange it."

"Yes, Father," Pio said, dragging himself to his feet. Both men looked at the pile of wires and microphones still lying on Father Romano's desk.

"I don't know if we'll ever get to the bottom of this, Pio. It's unlikely anyone will ever fess up to doing such an awful thing."

Father Romano was right. Nobody ever did admit to wiretapping the confessional.

After Father Romano's call to the hospital board, word of what had happened spread quickly. When Pio met with the board at the hospital one evening later that week to announce his resignation, the hallway was thronged with supporters: townspeople, parishioners, doctors, even the Mayor of San Giovanni Rotondo was present. The place was in an uproar.

"Fight back, Padre!" people called out.

"Pio, you can't take this lying down!" said Dr. Sanguinetti. "This was your dream! Don't let them rob you!"

There was jostling, arguing, and commotion as the people tried to convince Padre Pio to strike back against his accusers.

The mayor stepped forward, handing Pio a flyer. "I'm having this printed in the newspaper," he said proudly. The flyer was an angry attack against the Church hierarchy, ridiculing the bishops and Capuchin superiors for their treatment of Pio.

Pio's faced flushed red. He crumpled the paper up and threw it at the mayor's feet. "Satan!" he shouted, shaking his finger in the man's face. The room fell silent as the man shrunk back. Pio grabbed him by the collar like a parent seizing a wayward child. "Who do you think you are? Go and throw yourself at the feet of the Church instead of writing this foolishness! Don't oppose your mother!"

The mayor was speechless, having been reduced to a quaking mass of jelly at the unexpected berating of the friar. Pio let him go and turned to the others. "Have you all learned nothing? Shall we accept the good from God and not the bad? Who are *we*? Dust and ashes! We are but dust and ashes!" his voice wavered with passion, his tone a mixture of anger and tortured pain. "Go and learn humility!"

The mayor picked up the crumpled flyer and sulked out the door into the night. One by one, the people drained out, emptying the hall. Pio leaned against the wall and sunk down onto the floor, burying his head in his knees. He tried to pray but exhaustion overcame him. His mind bled into a loose stream of consciousness—prayers, thoughts, memories, and feelings all swirling together. He felt how he'd felt as a boy after cutting up Andrianella Brambilla's ribbon, when he sobbed in the alfalfa pile. Then through the gleaming mist of half-forgotten dreams and ancient memory, he recalled his father smiling at him in the pink rays of the dawn over the plains, telling him, "The true battle is against yourself."

"Every man alone with God," he muttered as sleep overtook his weary, broken frame.

CHAPTER 13

The Embroidery of Life

FORTUNATELY, THE NEW prohibitions against Padre Pio were not enforced for long. Pope John XXIII was soon dead, and the new pope—Paul VI—was an admirer of Padre Pio. Paul VI lifted every restriction on Padre Pio's life and ministry, and the monks of San Giovanni Rotondo were not disbanded. For the rest of his days, Pio and the Capuchins would have no more trouble from the Church authorities.

But that's not to say things calmed down for Pio. Even in old age, his life was an unrelenting surge of activity: matters of the hospital to attend to, pilgrims to be greeted, letters to be answered, confessions to be heard, Masses to be celebrated, prayer groups needing spiritual direction, and a host of other duties—and this on top of his regular observance of Capuchin life within the friary.

Through it all, Pio never allowed himself to become too distracted with human affairs. The spiritual world was ever present, existing behind the world of the senses. As always, his rosary was constantly in his hand. The old friar committed all things to Christ and Mary, spoke intimately with his guardian angel as to a friend, and, above and beyond all things, he saw the beneficent hand of God governing it all according to his mysterious purposes.

One day, Pio was saying Mass in San Giovanni Rotondo when three men entered, dragging in an elderly woman who struggled violently to free herself from their grasp. When she passed over the threshold and entered into the sanctuary, she began to shake and cry out. The parishioners gawked but remained silent, trying to be polite. "Perhaps she has an illness," they muttered.

Pio knew better. From his place at the altar, he could see a dark creature clinging to the back of the old woman. He recognized the presence of the Enemy. This woman was possessed.

Pio attempted to complete the Mass, despite the woman's random outbursts. The other parishioners shifted about uncomfortably, trying to focus and pretend as if they were not terribly distracted. At Holy Communion, however, the woman became so enraged it was impossible to ignore. She swung her hands wildly as the three men attempted to restrain her. "Mother! Mother, please!" they kept saying. It seemed these men were her sons. But she easily overpowered them as a litany of blasphemies and curses flooded out of her mouth. The parishioners began to cry out in fear.

"Get out of here! This is no place for you!" he yelled, speaking not to the woman but to the creature clinging to her back.

The woman scowled at the priest with a perverse, twisted grin. "I'd rather die than leave!" she hissed, spittle flying from her mouth.

"Padre Pio, help our poor mother!" one of the men called. "She's being tormented by a demon!"

The old woman turned and slapped the man, far harder than one could think possible considering her small frame. The *crack* of the slap reverberated through the sanctuary as the man spun around and fell over. "Shut your mouth, idiot!" the woman screamed.

Pio had enough. He took the Sacred Host in his hands and elevated it, facing the direction of the woman. "This ends now!" he called out, his voice deep and resonant. Instantly, the woman collapsed to the floor, still and silent. All the commotion ceased. The congregation stared at the motionless hulk on the floor. They couldn't help wondering if she was dead, but Pio knew better. The demon had left her. He smiled, then turned back to the altar to continue the Mass. "*Domine Jesu Christe, qui dixísti Apóstolis tuis: Pacem relínquo vobis, pacem mean do vobis . . .*" As Pio went on with the liturgy, speaking of the peace of Christ, the woman slowly pulled herself up, looked around, and blinked. Her sons ran to help her to her feet. She patted her hair as if suddenly self-conscious. Her sons led her to a pew against the back wall and sat with her silently while Pio finished the Mass.

After Mass ended, the woman and her sons were thronged with people wanting to know their story. Pio knew there would be a commotion, and so he slipped out of the church by the back door. He was never comfortable in crowds but especially not when something like this happened. Still, these days there was no solitude for Pio. When he entered the street, he was immediately surrounded by a horde of people, many whom had come to San Giovanni Rotondo from far away, in hopes of catching a glimpse of Pio.

"Padre! Bless my children!" a woman cried, dragging her wiggling toddlers across the road to the priest. Pio put his gloved hand on their heads and pronounced a priestly benediction.

Another woman thrust a letter into his hand, "Padre, I am in need of spiritual advice. Will you please read this when you have time?"

"Eh . . . yes, I will try," said Pio, forcing a tired smile.

"Padre!" a man called, touching his shoulder. "My father is very ill, can you remember him in your prayers? His name is Giuseppe. Will you remember? Giuseppe."

"Look! There's Padre Pio!" a woman on the street called out in a French accent as she approached. So many people were speaking at once, waving letters, just trying to touch him. The old friar could not discern everything that was being said to him. It sounded like a cacophonous babble. He merely smiled, nodded, and raised his gloved hand in blessing again and again. "Pray, hope, and don't worry," he said as people poured their troubles out to him.

"Come, Padre," came a familiar voice cutting through the clatter. It was Fra Giorgio, one of the friars assigned to Padre Pio to help get him from place to place. "Thank you everyone," said Fra Giorgio, collecting their letters with one hand whilst moving Pio along with the other. "Padre will read all of your letters and pray for all of you."

When they had left the crowd behind, Pio said, "Thank you, Giorgio. I was beginning to feel overwhelmed."

"That's why you shouldn't sneak out of the church without me, Padre," said Giorgio. When they reached the monastery, he added, "Go rest in your cell, Padre. I will come get you for vespers."

"Thank you, Giorgio."

The brother left the stack of letters on Pio's desk before leaving. His body drenched in sweat, Pio laid upon his cot and put his feet up, groaning. He closed his eyes. "Just a moment's rest," he said to himself. "Not too long. 'Give no occasion to the flesh,'" he mumbled, quoting Saint Paul as his heavy eyelids dropped.

Just as he drifted off, Pio was abruptly awakened by a knock on his door. He sat up, unsure if he had been asleep for seconds or days. The door creaked open. It was a friar with two workmen. "Sorry for disturbing you, Padre," said the friar. "We are here to install one of these new air conditioning units in your cell."

"What?" Pio said bewildered.

"Father Superior has ordered that every cell have one of these air conditioning units. Now you won't have to lay here and sweat. Isn't that wonderful?"

Pio sat up. "Air conditioning? I didn't choose the Capuchins for a life of ease. What would Saint Francis say?"

"Well . . . I, ah . . . I don't know, but Father Superior says—"

"—Good Lord," Pio said, crossing himself, "I have lived too long!"

"Maybe we should just come back later," the friar said to the workmen, hustling them out of the room. "Sorry to disturb you, Padre," he said before shutting the door.

The following day, a message came from the Superior, dispensing Pio from having to use an air conditioner. He would be allowed to continue to sweat in his cell as he wished.

As was made evident by the episode with the air conditioning, Pio was feeling increasingly out of touch with things. Everything was changing, becoming new and mechanized, a world of machines and plastic—and *noise*. One could no longer walk up the cobblestone streets of San Giovanni Rotondo without being overwhelmed. One of the main causes was due to pedestrians being forced to yield the road to automobiles, which rumbled incessantly through the town with their clamor and fumes. Electrical wires were also now strung from giant poles lining the streets, their transistors filling the air with a dull, persistent hum. Radios blared from storefronts, and televisions had begun to appear; Pio even heard that there were monasteries where monks spent their free time gathered around this new glowing box.

Pio's own monastery itself had been remodeled and modernized as well. Even the farmlands were changing; the sunbaked laborers that had pushed plows behind mules and oxen since Roman times were disappearing, giving way to gigantic, mechanized tractors. Generations of peasant farmers like his father had once carved furrows in the earth by the sweat of their brow; now, the new machines mindlessly tore the ground with factory efficiency. It was a strange new world indeed.

In 1968, as the heat of summer yielded to fall and the blue Campanian sky became a little grayer, the fig and olive leaves turned a crisp yellow, giving the appearance of hillsides swathed in golden clusters. Below on the plains, little fleets of mechanized reapers and threshers zigzagged across the fields, doing the job Pio and his father used to do with a scythe and a ball of twine.

For the old friar, it was a special anniversary.

"It's been fifty years now since I have received these wounds," he said to his personal physician, Dr. Sala. He peeled his black gloves off and showed them to the doctor. Sala held the old man's hands in his own, examining the wounds. "Can you believe it? Fifty years."

The doctor stared intently at the red wounds on the palms of Pio's hands. "You know, Padre," he said, "I might be seeing things, but I think they are healing."

"What?" said Pio in disbelief, looking down at his hands. "Impossible. They've been fresh for fifty years."

"Yes, yes, but I'm sure of it. I've been looking at your wounds for ten years now, since your superiors commanded you to have regular checkups, and I am quite certain the hole in your hand has shrunken a bit. May I see your feet?"

Pio removed his cracked leather sandals, peeled off the sweaty black woolen socks that hid his feet from prying eyes, and unwrapped his bloody bandages. Dr. Sala lifted Pio's gnarled feet and stared at them through thick spectacles.

"Pio, the wounds on your feet, they're almost gone!"

"*Non mi dire*!" Pio exclaimed. "Really?"

"Plain as day," said Sala. "Look for yourself."

Pio lifted his leg and examined the sole of his foot. Dr. Sala was not wrong. The wound had almost vanished; the only evidence of the painful, bloody wound was a small red spot on the skin, almost like a circular rash. Pio poked it with his finger

"It doesn't even hurt anymore." He looked at the bloody bandages, puzzled. "I wrapped these only a few days ago."

Sala examined Pio's side as well, and there, too, the bloody wound that had afflicted him for so many years was shrinking. "It looks to me like you're healing up, Pio," the doctor concluded. "I can't say why."

Dr. Sala went on to offer several medical explanations for why Pio's wounds of fifty years were suddenly healing, but Pio instinctively knew the truth of the matter.

My time is almost up.

That September, San Giovanni Rotondo was crowded with visitors from all over the world for an international prayer meeting. The little prayer groups Padre Pio had been encouraging for years had blossomed, blooming into a global community numbering in the tens of thousands. They had all converged upon San Giovanni Rotondo to honor the founder of their prayer movement and to be with Pio for the fiftieth anniversary of his stigmata. It was a busy time for Pio: extra Masses, confessions, the blessing of a new Stations of the Cross, meetings with leaders of the prayer groups. It all wore on the old man's strength even as it nurtured his soul.

On September 22, Pio rose early to celebrate Mass at 5 a.m. At eighty-one years old, Pio looked frail and weak. He leaned upon Fra Giorgio for help as he ascended to the altar. His body seemed to sink beneath the weight of his clerical vestments as he made the sign of the cross. *"Introíbo ad altáre Dei,"* he said weakly—"I will go in to the altar of God." Fra Giorgio, acting as his server, responded, *"Ad Deum qui lætíficat juventútem meam*—to God who gives joy to my youth."

Ah, the joy of my youth! thought Pio.

Now, at the twilight of life, his youth seemed remote like a half-remembered dream from another time, vanished upon waking and forever irretrievable. Still, he knew the Psalm did not refer only to physical youth but to the endless happiness of heaven. He imagined his youth renewed, leaping over hills like a gazelle in the joy of heaven, every tear wiped away under the smile of God.

Pio genuflected before the altar. His knees burned, his muscles ached. The very act of walking to the church had exhausted him. He saw his fingers trembling as he placed them upon the altar to steady himself. He felt out of sorts, as if his mind and soul were elsewhere. He sung the Mass, but his voice wavered as if he struggled to find it.

The strange feeling only intensified as the Mass went on, until Pio felt delirious by the end. "Jesus, help me," he whispered. When he finally completed the celebration and turned to leave the altar, his feet gave out beneath him. He collapsed into the arms of Fra Giorgio. The congregation leapt up. "My children! My children!" he cried out. A group of friars and laypersons thronged about Pio. He stared up at their faces. They all seemed blurry, formless, otherworldly. He could not make anyone out.

"Padre, Padre, stay with me," said Fra Giorgio, gently tapping Pio's cheek. Pio looked up at the friar and squinted.

"Is that you, Giorgio?"

"Yes, Padre, it's me." Giorgio's face came into focus. "Are you all right?"

"Yes, I—I think so. I just had a fainting spell."

Giorgio helped Pio out of his vestments and returned him to his chambers. Pio spent most of that day in his cell, praying and sleeping and moving imperceptibly between the two states. He rested on his back, clutching a crucifix he held upon his chest, his other hand turning the beads of his well-worn rosary. His breathing was difficult, wispy with a wheezing scratch.

Later that evening, Pio awoke to the sound of singing. It was distant, wafting in the air like a breeze. He struggled to focus. *Who is singing?* It seemed to be coming from outside. He sat up and shuffled over the small window, his cell's sole portal to the outer world. A crowd had gathered outside the monastery, holding candles, singing, and praying, all for him. A surge of emotion welled up inside Pio. Tears moistened his tired eyes. For a brief moment, he could actually *feel* their prayers, feel them lifting his spirit even as his body faded like being propped up by ten thousand hands.

A man outside caught sight of him. "It's Padre Pio!" he cried. Everyone gazed at the monk through the window in awe. Pio suddenly felt awkward and exposed. He smiled weakly, waved a gloved hand at his admirers and hastily blessed them before disappearing back into the shadow of his cell. But he did not feel alone—there was someone in the room with him. Whirling around, he saw what seemed to be a young boy, dark-eyed and curly haired standing before him.

"Hello, Francesco," the boy said in a thin, tinny voice.

"It's Pio to you," Padre Pio answered testily. "And it's no use! I remember you, and I know your tricks! You'd might as well flee."

"I couldn't let you go without saying goodbye," the boy replied sarcastically.

"It's never too soon to say goodbye to you," scoffed Pio, making the sign of the cross. The priest turned and clambered back to his bed.

But the boy followed him. "Doesn't it make you angry? What benefit has serving God brought you? What do you have to show for all these years?"

"Go away!"

"Think of all your troubles," hissed the boy. "Raised in poverty—so poor your papa had to abandon you to go to America *twice* just to support you and your brood! No natural gifts! You're nothing to look at, no talent, and you've always been a *stupido.*"

"Bah," Pio grunted, waving the boy away.

"Misunderstood and teased by the village boys! Couldn't even have a normal novitiate because you were always sick. Then the Church you vowed to serve has done nothing but crush and humiliate you. And those, those *things* on your hands and feet have been nothing but endless pain and suffering. What about those maniacs outside, eh? They don't know you. They don't love you. They are infatuated with you because you titillate them and scratch some kind of itch for novelty inside their sloppy, foolish lives. You're a curiosity—a circus freak! And once you're gone, they'll forget you entirely and move on to the next thing. You mean nothing. Your work means nothing. Your life has meant nothing. What has all this suffering brought you? God has done nothing for you!"

"Are you finished yet?" asked Pio, stretching out on his cot. "I'm tired, and I need to lay down."

The face of the boy twisted in an expression of contempt and defeat. Pio blew at him as if blowing out a candle. The apparition of the boy dissolved into a thousand tiny black grains of shadow and vanished. Pio grunted, and taking up his crucifix, prayed the forty-fourth Psalm: "Thou art my King and my God, who ordains victories for Jacob. Through thee we push down our foes; through thy name, we tread down our assailants. For not in my bow do I trust, nor can my sword save me. But thou hast saved us from our foes and hast put to confusion those who hate us."

Around midnight, Fra Giorgio came to check on Padre Pio. The old man was sweating profusely and shaking. "Giorgio," Pio wheezed, "would you be so kind as to get one of the other padres to say my Mass in the morning? I'm afraid I won't be able to."

"Of course, Padre. You need your rest."

"There's no time for rest now, Giorgio. This is the end."

"What do you mean? You just have a fever. You'll be fine in no time."

"Giorgio, the sufferings in my life, the trials we all receive from the hand of God, they do have purpose." He stared at Giorgio, a profound gaze from his deep brown eyes, his forehead beaded with sweat. His look was odd, almost as if he were looking *through* Giorgio instead of at him. The friar got the sense that Pio was talking to someone else, picking up some previous conversation of which Giorgio was unaware.

"Is that so, Padre?" Giorgio said politely to mask his confusion.

"I'll tell you how it is. A lady was embroidering a beautiful pattern. Her small son was seated beside her on a low stool. He saw her work but only from the back side. Seeing only the knots and the tangled threads of the embroidery, he asked, 'Mother, what are you doing? I can't make out what you are doing!' Then the mother lowered the embroidery hoop and showed him the beautiful pattern of her work. Each color was in its proper place, the various threads forming a harmonious design. So, too, we see the reverse of the embroidery of our lives because we are seated on a low stool. Things will look different when we see it from the other side."

Giorgio nodded. "That's very profound, Padre."

"Profound?" Pio shrugged. "It's simply the truth. No suffering borne out of love for Christ, even poorly borne, will go unrewarded in eternal life. Even poor clay—" he thumped his hand against his chest violently "—even this poor clay will become finest gold which will shine in the palace of heaven!"

His thought was interrupted by a fit of shaking and coughing. "Giorgio, my son, go fetch one of the padres to hear my confession," Pio wheezed between fits.

Giorgio dashed off down the darkened corridor. That night, Pio made his last confession and received Last Rites. As the sun rose, casting its pink drapery over the Campanian hills, the friars of Our Lady for Grace gathered in Pio's cell to pray and say their goodbyes.

"Pray for my poor soul," begged Pio, "and forgive me for all the trouble I have caused you all." The friars wept and assured him there was nothing to forgive. As Pio lay suffering, he looked about the room. The faces were familiar from chapel and table, but all his dear old friends were gone. *Padre Agostino, Padre Benedetto, both passed. Father Serelli. Fra Camillo. I'm the last.* Then he cast his mind back even further, to his days at home in Pietrelcina. *My father, Mamma Peppa, Michele. All gone. I am ready to see them. I am ready to see Jesus.*

At the thought of his mother, Pio turned his eyes to the yellowed old photo of the woman he kept hanging on his wall. Her gaze was both loving and stoic, in a way only Italian women are. The black and white expression stared out at him from another time. He smiled weakly at her memory. But then beside the face of Mamma Peppa, he saw another woman—smiling, radiant, beaming grace from her pure countenance. Her appearance was welcoming, almost beckoning, and Pio felt called out of himself as if pulled. His face lit up. "I see two mothers!" he cried.

"You're not seeing well, Padre," said Fra Giorgio. "There is only one picture on your wall."

"Don't worry about me," Pio whispered. "I see very well, and there are two mothers." His eyes widened. A look of peace flooded him. "Jesu! María! Jesu! María!" he repeated. His forehead beaded with sweat. The friars closed in around his bed, intoning the requiem *Media vita in morte sumus*. By the time the chant had ended, Pio's head was bowled over, his sagging eyelids closed.

The Father Superior leaned in, placing his ear to Pio's mouth. "No breath," he said solemnly. "Padre Pio has passed."

The friars burst into tears, petrified with grief at the loss of their beloved Pio. Others knelt on the floor of the cell, saying prayers for Pio's soul, though few had any doubts he was already reposing in endless light.

Fra Giorgio approached the body, struggling to maintain his composure, his lips quivering. He lovingly positioned Pio's head upon the center of his pillow, wiped his brow, and straightened his legs. Day was dawning, and many would want to come in and pay their respects. Giorgio wanted to arrange the body in such a way to make it suitable for viewing. He picked up Pio's arms and crossed them upon his chest. At the sight of the gloved hands, Giorgio hesitated. He turned and looked at the Father Superior. Father Superior knew what Giorgio was thinking.

"Remove the gloves, Giorgio," he said. "Let us all finally look upon that which Pio guarded during his life."

The friars gathered around the bed, clustered about the body in a strange mixture of grief and childlike curiosity. Giorgio peeled the sweaty, fingerless gloves off the old man's hands and laid his palms face up for the sight of all.

The friars gasped. The wounds were gone, save for a slight red discoloration on the palms and the backs of the hands. The friars could hardly contain their consternation. "What does this mean?" they whispered. "How could this be?"

Giorgio sunk down on his knees, heaving with anxiety. "I . . . I . . . I saw them last month when I was helping him dress! I don't understand. Holes like that don't simply vanish."

"God does as he pleases," said the Father Superior, nodding as if in deference to a mystery light years beyond his understanding. And as he did, in the sight of all, the little red marks vanished, leaving Pio's skin fresh, uniform, as smooth as any child's on the day of his birth.

Afterword

Padre Pio died on the morning of September 23, 1968. News of his death spread quickly, and the people of San Giovanni Rotondo were grief-stricken. Crowds filled the town square and the church to pray and share memories of their blessed Pio. They clutched their rosaries; those who were unable to pray simply held their beads and wept. The townspeople felt as if their own father had been taken.

Padre Pio's body was thoroughly examined after his death. All signs of the stigmata had vanished. Dr. Sala, Pio's superiors, and others who had witnessed the wounds all gave testimonies as to what they had seen. Dr. Sala confirmed that Pio's wounds had begun to heal in the months leading up to his death. Father Superior noted that Pio had often expressed his desire that God take the wounds from him before his death and that the mystery was a sign that God had heard his prayer.

Pio's funeral was held four days later. Never had so many come to San Giovanni Rotondo; local officials estimated as many as 100,000 persons came through the town that week to bid farewell to the beloved Capuchin saint. A procession of mourners five miles long stretched from the church through the town out into the countryside. A requiem Mass was said, and Pio's remains were solemnly blessed before being interred in the monastery crypt.

Despite Pio's fame, there were still those who thought ill of him. "Now that he's gone, this whole business at San Giovanni Rotondo will die out," they predicted. The opposite proved true. Pilgrims continued to flock to San Giovanni Rotondo. *Casa Sollievo della Sofferenza* flourished and was enlarged multiple times, eventually becoming a massive complex that dominated the slopes of Mount Gargano. Business came to San Giovanni Rotondo to serve the flood of pilgrims: restaurants, hotels, stores, and more. A new church was constructed to accommodate the pilgrims, capable of seating 6,000 people (with standing room for another 10,000). The sprawling pilgrim church contains multiple chapels, confessionals, a service center, and offices. Meanwhile, his prayer groups continued to flourish worldwide as the reputation of Padre Pio continues to grow to this day.

One could debate whether Padre Pio would approve of such noise and fuss being made about him if he were here—thankfully, he is in heaven and has a much better view of things, looking from "the other side of the embroidery." How do we know he is in heaven? On May 2, 1999, Pope Saint John Paul II beatified Padre Pio; he was canonized three years later, on June 16, 2002. His feast day is September 23, the day of his birth into eternal life.

At the canonization, John Paul II said, "The life and mission of Padre Pio prove that difficulties and sorrows, if accepted out of love, are transformed into a privileged way of holiness, which opens onto the horizons of a greater good, known only to the Lord. Is it not, precisely, the glory of the Cross that shines above all in Padre Pio? How timely is the spirituality of the Cross lived by the humble Capuchin of Pietrelcina. Our time needs to rediscover the value of the Cross in order to open the heart to hope. Throughout his life, he always sought greater conformity with the Crucified, since he was very conscious of having been called to collaborate in a special way in the work of redemption. His holiness cannot be understood without this constant reference to the Cross."

Since then, Saint Padre Pio has been among the most popular and beloved modern saints. His face is universally recognized, and to this day millions of pilgrims stream through the Campanian town of San Giovanni Rotondo yearly to honor and connect with the humble Capuchin friar. And what of Pio himself? After his canonization, his body was interred in a glass case in the shrine of San Giovanni Rotondo. Still clothed in his Capuchin habit, his body lies in repose, gloved hands crossed on his breast, clutching a crucifix as Giorgio had left him. There, his mortal frame awaits the resounding of the last trumpet and the voice of the Son of Man that will raise the dead, when "mortality will be clothed in immortality" (1 Cor 15:54).